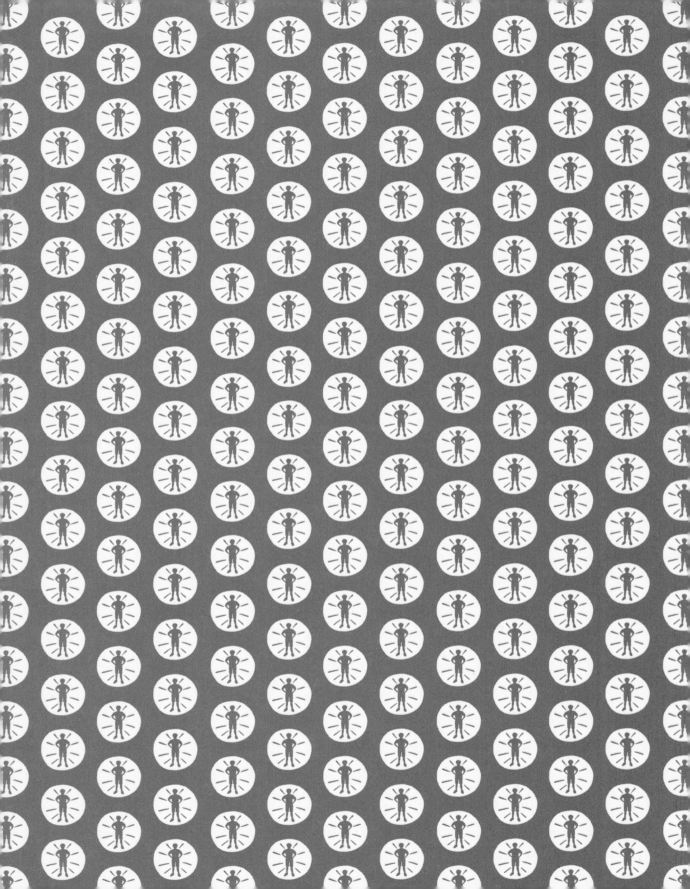

# STORIES FOR BOYS WHO DARE TO BE DIFFERENT

Running Press Kids
Hachette Book Group
1290 Avenue of the Americas, New York, NY 10104
www.runningpress.com/rpkids
@RP_Kids

Made in Malaysia

Originally published in Great Britain in 2018 by Quercus Editions Ltd, a Hachette UK company

First U.S. Edition: September 2018

Published by Running Press Kids, an imprint of Perseus Books, LLC, a subsidiary of Hachette Book Group, Inc. The Running Press Kids name and logo is a trademark of the Hachette Book Group.

The Hachette Speakers Bureau provides a wide range of authors for speaking events. To find out more, go to www.hachettespeakersbureau.com or call (866) 376-6591.

The publisher is not responsible for websites (or their content) that are not owned by the publisher.

Illustrations by Quinton Winter.
Print book cover design by Arnauld.

Library of Congress Control Number: 2018938087

ISBNs: 978-0-7624-6592-7 (hardcover),
978-0-7624-6591-0 (ebook)

IM

10  9  8

# STORIES FOR BOYS WHO DARE TO BE DIFFERENT

## TRUE TALES OF AMAZING BOYS WHO CHANGED THE WORLD WITHOUT KILLING DRAGONS

### Ben Brooks

ILLUSTRATED BY QUINTON WINTER

RP | KIDS

PHILADELPHIA

# CONTENTS

# PATCH ADAMS

## (BORN 1945)

Patch was bullied at school for being different and for standing up to the racism that he saw around him. Because of the bullying, he ended up in the hospital three times. On his third visit, when Patch was eighteen, he decided that, after he got out, he'd start a revolution to spread happiness.

For a while, he found it difficult to be around people, so he set out to do experiments in friendliness. He would call random numbers on his phone and speak to the people on the other end until they'd become friends. He would start up conversations with strangers in the street. And he would ride elevators up as many floors as it took for the people inside to introduce themselves and start laughing together.

Patch became a clown and a doctor. He started his own hospital called the Gesundheit! Institute, where his goal wasn't just to make his patients less sick, but to make them happier, too.

These days, he flies all over the world, giving talks and performances as a clown and as a doctor. Patch doesn't think the two jobs have to be separate.

To him, laughter is one of the best medicines. It can get the blood flowing, strengthen your heart, and even help your body fight off diseases.

If you want to help make the world a better place, Patch has some suggestions: be silly in public, wear funny clothes, be friendly to everyone you meet, and pick up all the garbage that you see in your town.

"Anyone can do something," he says. "It's about deciding to do it—to dive into work for peace and justice and care for everybody on the planet."

# EDDIE AIKAU

## (1946–1978)

Eddie surfed whenever he could. Before school, after school, and sometimes even during school, if he could get away. He lived on Oahu, the third largest Hawaiian island, and the ocean meant everything to him.

Working at a pineapple factory was how Eddie saved up enough money for his first surfboard. After that, he got a job as a lifeguard and was given the task of covering all the beaches on the North Shore of the island.

Even though the waves could sometimes rise as tall as utility poles, not a single person was lost on Eddie's patch while he was lifeguard. He would venture out into waves that no one else would dare go near. Eddie never let the sea take anyone away. For that, they made him Lifeguard of the Year.

One day, Eddie joined a crew on a wooden boat to re-enact the historic journey taken by Polynesian migrants between the Hawaiian and Tahitian islands. They would travel using traditional methods and navigate only by the sun and stars.

They ran into terrible weather. The water was so rough that it capsized the ship, tossing everyone overboard. Desperately, they clung to the sides of the boat, trying to stay afloat.

"Don't worry," Eddie told the crew. "I'll go and get help."

He swam away, into the dark, rolling sea.

The crew was eventually rescued. Nobody ever saw or heard from Eddie again.

To this day, when faced with tall waves or stormy weather, Hawaiian surfers say to each other, "Eddie would go." Every year, they hold a surfing competition in his honor. They cancel frequently because they only go ahead if the waves are huge.

# DR. NAIF AL-MUTAWA

In 1979, Naif spent his summer at Camp Robin Hood, on the edge of a giant lake in America. That was where he first opened a comic book and lost himself in a world of superheroes.

Back home in Kuwait, Naif realized that there were no Muslim characters in any of the comic books he was reading. He decided that he would grow up to be a writer, so he could create them, but his father told him to study a more practical subject. Naif agreed, but he never forgot his dream.

In 2007, he made it a reality.

The 99 are a team of superheroes from all around the world, each named after one of the different ninety-nine qualities of Allah, which is the Muslim name for God.

They get their powers after finding magic stones that have been secretly scattered around the world hundreds of years earlier. The stones were created by the librarians of Baghdad, to preserve the city's wisdom after it was destroyed by invaders.

One character, Mujiba the Responder, has answers to everything, and wears a headscarf like a lot of Muslim girls.

Another character, Darr the Afflicter, uses a wheelchair and can manipulate people's nerves.

The 99 battle their enemies without violence. Like their religion, they teach peace.

Naif wanted to give Muslim boys and girls their own superheroes. He also wanted the world to have a deeper understanding of Islam than what is sometimes shown on the news.

The comics have sold thousands of copies, been turned into a TV show, and are handed out to children at refugee camps.

Naif has received death threats because of the 99. But he's also been praised. President Obama thanked him for inspiring so many young Muslims and for letting them know that they can be superheroes, too.

# MOHED ALTRAD

## (BORN 1948)

Mohed grew up in a tribe that would chase the rains across the Syrian Desert. Wherever the rains were, plants would grow, which meant the tribe's goats, camels, and sheep would have something to eat.

It was a difficult life. Mohed's mother died young, followed by his brother, and his dad wouldn't speak to him at all. He was raised by his grandma, who told him that he'd grow up to be a shepherd.

"But I want to go to school," he told her, one day.

"Don't be silly," she said. "Shepherds don't go to school."

Mohed didn't listen. In the mornings, he'd secretly race barefoot across the hot desert sand to a schoolhouse, where the other kids would bully him for being poor. He ignored them, knowing education was his only chance to get out.

He worked so hard, he won a place to go to France and study. Once he arrived, Mohed realized he could hardly understand anything the teachers said, and he was so poor he could only afford to eat once a day.

Still, he carried on working until his French got better and he graduated with a degree that helped him find a job.

Mohed saved and saved and bought a company that was about to fall apart. He renamed the company after himself—Altrad—and he turned it around. Today, it has 1 million customers, in 100 countries, and 17,000 employees to organize everything.

Mohed's proven, to himself and everyone else, that it doesn't matter how you grow up, or what people tell you you're supposed to be—there are no limits to what you can achieve.

# ROALD AMUNDSEN

## (1872–1928)

As a boy, Roald dreamed of being an explorer.
He would picture himself trekking across the vast uncharted
polar wilderness and imagine himself becoming the first
person ever to reach the North Pole.

But it was never going to happen. His mother made him promise that he wouldn't go off on dangerous adventures, and that he would study medicine and become a doctor instead.

"Okay," Roald told her. "I won't go."

When she died, Roald was devastated, but he decided he could finally become an explorer. To prepare for his journeys, he slept with all his windows open during the freezing winter. He also made visits to native people living in the north. They taught him about wearing animal skins against the cold and using dogs to drag sleds across the snow.

It was hard work, but Roald still wanted to be the first person at the North Pole. He put all his energy into preparing an expedition. Then, one day, terrible news came: a man named Robert Peary had beaten him to it.

Not wanting to give up, Roald secretly turned his expedition around and tried to become the first person to reach the South Pole instead. It would be difficult. There was already a famous English explorer named Captain Scott trying to get there, and he'd had a head start.

But Roald was faster.

With four people, four sleds, fifty-two dogs, and lots of determination, he became the first person to reach the South Pole.

Using his new fame, Roald built a huge airship and flew to the North Pole to fulfil his dream. Later, people found out that Robert Peary had never actually been there. In the end, Roald was first to the North Pole, after all.

# DANIEL ANTHONY

## (1794–1862)

During the first half of the nineteenth century,
Susan came home from school one day and explained
that she wasn't being taught long division.
Her dad was furious.

"Why not?" he wanted to know. "How can you not be learning math?"

She wasn't being taught it because her teacher was refusing to teach it to girls; he would only teach it to the boys. So Daniel, Susan's father, immediately opened his own school where anyone could learn about anything they wanted, regardless of gender.

Daniel ran a cotton mill and a small local store. Unlike most other people at the time, he refused to sell alcohol, which was what made the most money. When the community needed to build some new houses for the mill workers, everyone said he'd need to provide gin and wine if he wanted the men to help, but he refused and instead concocted a delicious lemonade; the workers came and helped, anyway, and the houses were built without any drunken accidents.

Daniel was an abolitionist, which meant he wanted an end to slavery, and a pacifist, which meant he didn't believe in violence. He believed in hard work, family, and treating people equally, which are all values he tried to instill in his daughter.

It must have worked. Susan grew up to be one of the most important activists of the time. She campaigned for women's rights and against slavery, and was so effective and influential that, one hundred years later, her face was put on the dollar coin.

After her father died, Susan wrote to a friend saying, "The best way I could prove my love and respect for his memory, is to try to do more and better work for humanity than ever before."

And that's exactly what she did.

# LOUIS ARMSTRONG

## (1901–1971)

At ten years old, Louis had to drop out of school and start working to make money for his family. He sang in the street as well as working for a wealthy Jewish family, who were the first people to encourage his music. The Karnofskys gave him hot food, a warm bed, and even the money to buy his first instrument: a type of small trumpet called a cornet.

During a New Year's Eve party when he was eleven, Louis fired his stepdad's gun into the air and was arrested and sent to a special home for boys. At the home, Louis was given real guidance on how to play the cornet. Despite being alone, miserable, and away from his family, Louis managed to find joy and escape in music. By the time he left the home, he knew exactly what he wanted to do with the rest of his life.

Louis kept playing and was discovered and mentored by King Oliver, the most famous jazz cornet player of the time. Louis moved around and played music with whoever he could, wherever they were allowed.

During one recording session, Louis dropped the lyric sheet for the song. Instead of pausing, he carried on singing using made-up sounds. He'd accidentally invented a whole new type of performance: scat singing.

When the jazz bars started closing down because of the Depression, Louis was famous enough to tour around the world instead. He would perform up to three hundred concerts in a year and record hundreds of albums with the biggest bands around.

Louis still found time to spend with his family, even adopting his disabled nephew when his cousin passed away.

It was because of Louis that jazz music achieved the kind of popularity it did all over the world. One magazine called him, "America's greatest gift to the world."

In memory of the Karnofsky family, Louis always wore a Star of David and often blended Russian melodies into his music. He may have become one of the most famous musicians on the planet, but he wouldn't have been able to do any of it without that first little bit of encouragement.

# DAVID ATTENBOROUGH

## (BORN 1926)

David's parents were teachers, so he grew up on the grounds of a university, surrounded by traveling professors, thick books, and talk of fabulous new discoveries. What fascinated him most of all was the natural world, and he spent hours outside hunting for fossils, shells, and eggs.

David went to college to carry on his study of nature, then he joined the navy, hoping to catch a glimpse of it. Thrilled to finally venture out into world, he was annoyed when they only sent him as far as Wales!

Once he'd completed his service, he went to the BBC and asked if he could present shows about wildlife to the British public. The bosses were reluctant to put him on TV. There weren't many programs about the natural world, and they weren't sure that anyone would want to watch them. They also thought that David's teeth were too big and that no one would want to watch him either.

They couldn't have been more wrong.

Lying patiently in wait for days, weeks, and months, the film crews that have worked alongside David on his programs have caught some of the most beautiful shots of animals that have ever existed.

His shows have brought people face to face with gaping-mouthed anglerfish, illuminating the seabed with the glowing bulbs that hang from their heads. Viewers have seen sneaky cuckoos, slipping their own eggs into the nests of other birds. From the safety of their living rooms, they have even been able to watch lions chasing, catching, and feasting on zebras and gazelles.

David brought the exciting, magical, and bizarre world of nature into the homes of millions of viewers. And he wasn't just entertaining them; he was letting them know about the magnificent creatures with which we share our planet, the dangers those creatures face, and what we can do to help save them.

More than ten plants and animals have been named after David. When the British Antarctic Survey built a new ship to patrol the icy polar waters, they named that after him. too: the RRS *Sir David Attenborough*.

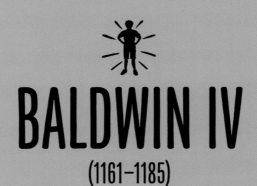

# BALDWIN IV

## (1161–1185)

In the year 1174, Baldwin's father died and Baldwin was crowned King of Jerusalem. He was thirteen years old. He also had leprosy, a disease that had no cure. People with leprosy tended to have shrunken fingers and toes, their hands and feet often needed to be cut off due to infection, and their eyes would darken until nothing could be seen out of them.

King Baldwin didn't let that stop him from riding out with his army. He always fought beside his men as if he was just as fit as they were.

Their biggest enemy was a sultan named Saladin, who ruled over Egypt, and Baldwin had put together a plan to attack his base in Cairo.

But the plan fell apart when Baldwin got sick and a lot of his allies left.

Saladin knew then that Jerusalem was weak. He seized this opportunity and sent his army of 26,000 men to take the town.

King Baldwin wouldn't let that happen. Not without a fight. He dragged himself out of bed and on to a horse. He was so unwell, one writer at the time described him as being "half dead." His bloody hands were wrapped in bandages and he could barely see through his swollen, cloudy eyes.

With only 500 men, he rode out to meet Saladin. But seeing how small the king's force was, Saladin ignored it completely and kept riding for Jerusalem. The people in the city were terrified, fearing for their homes and lives.

Baldwin prayed.

His men were afraid and outnumbered.

But, rallying his soldiers, King Baldwin led them into battle.

Somehow, they completely destroyed the invading forces: 500 men rescued their city from a force of 26,000. Jerusalem was saved.

Over 800 years later, a Hollywood film was made about the young king's triumph over Saladin. They called it *Kingdom of Heaven*.

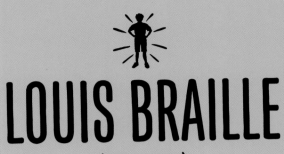

# LOUIS BRAILLE

## (1809–1852)

Louis was born in France in 1809, in a small house in the countryside, where his dad worked making saddles for horses. Louis loved watching him work. One day, he took down a tool and tried to copy what his dad was doing. The tool slipped and hit him in the face.

Louis became blind in both eyes.

He was sent to a school for the blind, where he proved that he was intelligent, but he got annoyed by how difficult things were for him.

Louis stayed at the school after graduating, becoming a professor and working with blind children. He wanted to improve their lives and he wanted people who didn't have eyesight problems to stop talking to them as though they were stupid or slow.

"We do not need pity," he said. "We must be treated as equals. And communication is how this can be brought about."

From a captain of the French army, Louis heard about something called night writing, which soldiers used to send messages without speaking on the battlefield. It was a series of raised dots and dashes that you could feel with your fingers.

Louis had an idea.

Using the very same tool that had blinded him, Louis began making small dots in paper. He created the system we now call Braille. It was easy to write, easy to read and easy to use in books.

Braille is now used by blind people all over the world. Famous musicians have learned to read music using it. New books are published in it. And it's been put on cash registers, museum exhibits, and traffic lights so that blind people have the freedom to live their lives like everyone else.

# EUGENE CERNAN

## (1934–2017)

Eugene Cernan was the last man to walk on the moon. Before going to space, he was just a young fighter pilot with the US Navy. He didn't apply for the space mission and hadn't gone to advanced pilot school, but for some reason NASA chose him.

At the time, he thought walking on the moon would be impossible. He'd never even considered going to space and he wasn't sure he was up to the challenge.

Ten years of training later, he got there. With his team, he roamed around the surface of the moon, staring back at the distant Earth while conducting experiments. They collected samples to learn about the moon's history, covered over twenty-one miles in the lunar rover, and even broke the unofficial moon land-speed record by going at eleven miles per hour!

The last thing he did before he left was to crouch and write his daughter's name in the dust: Tracy Dawn Cernan. Now it will stay there for over fifty thousand years.

Even though he was the last man on the moon, Eugene hoped it wouldn't stay that way. He thought it was sad that countries were no longer interested in reaching the moon and hoped that the next generation would be inspired to keep pushing the limits of space exploration. He wanted people to keep asking questions, seeking answers, and wondering what unsolved mysteries are waiting for us out in the cosmos.

"I'm quite disappointed that I'm still the last man on the moon," Eugene said before he died. Hopefully someone will change that soon.

# FAVIO CHÁVEZ

## (BORN 1975)

On the outskirts of Asunción, the capital city of Paraguay, lies a gigantic garbage dump called Cateura. Mountains and valleys made entirely of plastic bags and scrap metal stretch as far as the eye can see. Poor recyclers wander through those mountains and valleys, searching for small pieces of aluminium or plastic that they can trade in for a tiny bit of money.

As part of his job, Favio was hired to go to Cateura and teach the recyclers which things they should and shouldn't be looking for. While he was there, they got talking and he told them that he worked with a young people's orchestra in another town.

"Could you teach our children music, too?" the recyclers asked. "All they have to do while we work is hang around the dump. There's nothing for them here."

Favio thought about it. The problem was, a house in Cateura was worth less than a single violin, so for any of the kids to have one would be dangerous. But there was no way the kids would improve if they didn't have instruments on which to practice.

He decided that he and the recyclers could build their own instruments out of things that were thrown away. They used oil barrels, oven trays, and pieces of pipe to build flutes, cellos, and violins. The children were overjoyed. They practiced for two hours every day, and the Cateura Orchestra of Recycled Instruments was born.

The kids have now played in America, Norway, Palestine, and Japan, and the money they've made has been channeled back into their community built around a garbage dump. Through the power of music, Favio has brought hope into their lives.

# CONFUCIUS

## (551 BC–479 BC)

Confucius said, "Everything has beauty, but not everyone sees it."

He was born in China at a time when the country was being fought over by savage warlords who forced men into battle, others into work, and the rest into paying high taxes. As a teenager, he looked after farms nestled in the mountains. He spent his time thinking and coming up with ideas. When he became an adult, he left home to travel China, spreading his ideas.

Confucius said, "Wherever you go, go with all your heart."

He taught that leaders should lead by doing what's right and good, instead of chasing power or money. He said that those in power had a responsibility to look after their people. The warlords were against him, but their people felt like they had finally found someone who would speak for them.

Confucius said, "What you do not want done to yourself, do not do to others."

He returned to his homeland and opened a school, where he taught young people according to his beliefs: not just ethics and philosophy, but archery, calligraphy, and chariot-riding, too. His plan was to train the young men so that they could get jobs in government and change China for the better.

Confucius said, "Choose a job you love, and you will never have to work a day in your life."

Despite threats from vicious and violent warlords, Confucius never stopped speaking out for what he believed in. His teachings were so powerful and wise that people today still turn to them when they need guidance. You'll find them everywhere, from classrooms in England, to temples in Japan.

# FREDERICK DOUGLASS

## (1818–1895)

Frederick Douglass was born into slavery in America in 1818, which meant he was treated as property instead of a person. Slaves like Frederick were beaten, barely fed, and forced to work until they collapsed.

They were also banned from learning to read or write. The people who owned them were afraid that if their slaves became educated, they would rise up and overthrow them.

The wife of the man who owned Frederick ignored this rule, teaching Frederick how to read and write, until her husband found out and put a stop to it. He couldn't stop Frederick, though, who carried on learning whatever he could from local white children and neighbors, even though it put him in danger.

Once he could read, Frederick read everything: leaflets, newspapers, novels, the Bible. From reading, he learned about slavery and started to form his own ideas and arguments against what was happening. He shared these ideas with other slaves and his knowledge spread.

Frederick tried to escape from slavery twice, but was recaptured. He was successful on the third attempt, when he was transported along part of what was known as the Underground Railroad: a secret network of routes used to smuggle slaves to freedom.

As a free man, he married, had children, and traveled across America, speaking and campaigning, not just for the end of slavery, but for women's rights, Irish independence, and other issues he was passionate about. He advised presidents and lectured students. He also published three books about his life, which went on to be bestsellers.

Thanks in part to the work of Frederick, all slaves were declared free in 1865. Black people in America have been fighting for equality ever since.

# JESSE EISENBERG

## (BORN 1983)

During his first year of school, Jesse cried every day.
He hated it. He was nervous and sensitive and worried a lot
about everything. Being at school just made it worse.

"I don't want to go," he'd tell his parents every morning.

But he had to.

One day, someone asked if Jesse might like to try acting in a play. So he did. And everything changed.

For the duration of the play, he wasn't himself anymore. He was another character, lost in another world. He was Oliver Twist, darting through the grimy streets of London. Or the young Scrooge, helping the Ghost of Christmas Past teach his older self a lesson on Christmas Eve.

And he wasn't worried or nervous, because he was someone else. Being on stage and living out other people's lives felt like an escape because, inside the world of plays, he had control. Everyone knew what would happen next. And Jesse didn't feel so powerless.

So he moved to a school for art, music, dance, and drama, where he could focus on acting. Now, he stars in Hollywood films, writes books, and still puts together theater plays.

Jesse said that, when he grew up, he'd either be an astronaut or a banana. So far, he's already been a supervillain, a zombie hunter, a street magician, and a rare parrot named Blu.

Once, he was asked, "What would you tell the young Jesse about feeling worried and nervous?"

"It's not the worst thing in the world to have those feelings," he said. "Even though it might feel like it."

Why not? Because those feelings can come with positive qualities, like being sensitive and seeing the world differently from everyone else.

# JAIME ESCALANTE

## (1930–2010)

When Jaime went to teach math at Garfield High School, everyone said he was wasting his time. The school had a reputation for being violent and dangerous, and the students there often failed their exams or dropped out. Jaime didn't listen.

Both his parents had been teachers in Bolivia, where he'd grown up. He'd moved to America to build a better life for himself and he wanted to build better lives for his students, too.

Once he arrived at Garfield High, Jaime didn't start with simple math. Instead, he gave everyone the chance to learn complex equations. He told his students that education could be the key to their futures, if they only gave it a chance. If they would be patient and learn math, they could go on to get all kinds of jobs in electronics, computers, engineering, and science.

"You do not enter the future," he told them. "You create the future. The future is created through hard work."

The other teachers were distrustful of Jaime and his new methods. They thought he came to work too early and left too late. And they didn't approve of him making every student answer a question before they were allowed into the classroom. They may have been suspicious, but Jaime's methods showed amazing results.

"If he wants to teach us that bad," one student said, "then we can learn."

And they did.

The first year, two of his students passed the advanced math test, which no one from Garfield High had ever done before. The next year, nine passed. The year after that, so many of Jaime's students passed, the exam board thought they were cheating. They weren't. They'd just been inspired by a teacher who'd finally believed in them.

So many of his students got into the University of Southern California one year, they outnumbered all of the kids from the other local schools combined.

# THE FOUR CHAPLAINS

It was 1943, and an old luxury cruise liner called the *Dorchester* was carrying American army personnel through the icy waters of the Atlantic toward Greenland. A war was on. The captain knew there might be German submarines lurking out of sight and had ordered all 902 passengers to sleep with their life jackets on. Most were ignoring him.

They were spotted by a German U-boat. A few seconds later, three torpedoes tore through the ship. It rapidly began to sink below the arctic waters.

Everyone panicked. There was chaos. People rushed to deck, where freezing winds lashed their faces as they hurriedly packed themselves into lifeboats. It soon became clear that there wouldn't be enough room for all the soldiers.

Four army chaplains, all from different religions, remained calm. They tried to organize everyone and help get them away safely. They found more life jackets and handed them out. When there were none left, the chaplains took off their own and gave them away.

As the ship went down, the chaplains linked arms and stood on the deck praying. The people drifting away on lifeboats looked on in amazement and deep gratitude.

"It was the finest thing I have seen or hope to see this side of heaven," said one survivor.

# CHARLES FOURIER

## (1772–1837)

When his father died, Charles inherited enough money to leave home and travel all through Europe. He was excited to travel because he was a philosopher, which meant he spent most of his time thinking and writing, and the more he saw, the more he had to think and write about.

The point of all that thinking and writing was to try and make the world a better place for everyone in it. As he rattled through France in a horse-drawn carriage, Charles was thinking that an obvious way to do this would be to treat women better.

In his time, over two hundred years ago, women were treated a lot worse than men. They weren't allowed to own things or have jobs, or even vote in elections. Most of the time, they had to stay in the house, cleaning or cooking.

Charles didn't think this was right. He thought that we should all have the same opportunities in life, no matter what our gender. He wasn't the first person to think that, but he did invent a word for it, and that word stuck. The word was *feminism*, which really just means that boys and girls should be treated equally.

Since then, thanks to fights fought by a lot of brave women, we're much closer to equality than we were two hundred years ago.

Amazingly, though, we still have to use the word feminism because boys and girls aren't always treated the same. If you think they should be, then you can call yourself a feminist.

# GALILEO GALILEI

## (1564–1642)

Does the sun move around the earth?
Or does the earth move around the sun? How do you know?
Could you prove it?

Galileo could.

When he was young, his dad sent him to school to study medicine. It was going well until Galileo accidentally wandered into a math lecture and decided right then that he was going to devote his life to that instead. He believed that math and science would finally help us explain the world.

In Galileo's time, philosophers who came up with theories didn't really test them like the scientists of today. They'd simply come up with ideas, then announce they were true. One idea everyone believed in was that the earth was the center of the universe and the sun revolved around it.

Galileo disagreed.

Using a telescope he'd invented himself, Galileo had been studying our solar system. He'd discovered that the moon wasn't a smooth white ball but was covered in dark craters. And that four large moons circled Jupiter. He also found proof for his theory about Earth moving around the sun.

The Church wasn't happy with Galileo's findings, because they went against what was believed to be true. Galileo didn't mind. He kept carrying out his experiments anyway.

In one, he climbed to the very top of the Tower of Pisa and dropped two objects of different weights to the ground. Amazingly, even though one was far heavier, they both hit the floor at the same time. It went against what everyone believed.

That was the last straw for the Church, who thought that Galileo's ideas were making fun of God. They tried to sentence him to life in prison. When people protested, they put him under house arrest instead, which meant he wasn't allowed to leave his house for the rest of his life.

"We cannot teach people anything," Galileo said. "We can only help them discover it within themselves."

# MAHATMA GANDHI

## (1869–1948)

In 1858, after a vicious and bloody rebellion, the British army seized control of India. They brought some good things with them, like medicine and railways. But they also shot innocent Indians and caused millions to die from starvation.

Thirty years later, a nineteen-year-old man called Mahatma Gandhi traveled to England to study law. With his degree, he got a job and was sent with his family to work in South Africa.

Gandhi was shocked by the racism in South Africa. One day, he was beaten and thrown off a train for refusing to give up his seat to a white person.

This treatment led Gandhi to come up with a new type of action called satyagraha.

*Satyagraha* means "truth force," and using it means never allowing violence and only speaking the truth. According to Gandhi, nonviolence isn't being afraid to fight, it's just a different type of fighting. It's fighting with the heart and mind. It's fighting by refusing to hide, run, or attack with weapons.

Back in India, Gandhi taught his compatriots about this new tactic and they took it up to fight back against the British. They used protests, stopped buying British things, and ignored British laws that told them what they could and couldn't do.

In one protest, huge numbers of Indians turned out, quietly opposing the people who were ruling them. When they were arrested, they peacefully went to jails, and more people took their places. Eventually, the jails were so full, everyone had to be released.

Finally, in 1947, India gained its independence and the British sailed home.

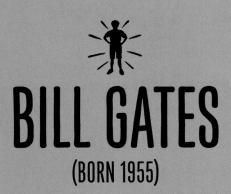

# BILL GATES

## (BORN 1955)

"There is no reason anyone would want a computer in their home," announced a rich businessman forty years ago.

Bill thought the opposite was true. He thought that, one day, every home in the world would have a computer. It seems obvious now, but it wasn't back then. At the time, computers were the size of ovens and couldn't do anything we'd find very exciting. They were so expensive that only big companies could afford to own them.

Bill was lucky, though; his school had made a deal with one of those companies, which meant the children were allowed to use their computer for a few hours every week.

Straight away, Bill was amazed by the possibilities. With his best friend, Paul Allen, Bill skipped classes and hid out in the computer room, hacking in to get more time. When he was only fifteen, he created a program that counted vehicle traffic, and he sold it for $20,000.

Once school was over, Bill's dad pressured him to go to college to study law. Bill went, but his heart wasn't really in it. All he could think about was computers. He kept imagining how they could become windows to everything we wanted to know about the world.

So he dropped out of college, called his old friend, Paul, and started a computer company called Microsoft.

Most of the computers in the world now use Microsoft. It's made Bill one of the richest people alive. To spend the money wisely, he started a charity with his wife, Melinda, and together they help people all over the world get access to clean water, food, disaster relief, education, medicine, and libraries.

# SIDDHARTHA GAUTAMA

## (CIRCA 480 BC–400 BC)

Gautama was a prince, born in a country called Nepal, in a grand palace surrounded by high walls. His parents, the king and queen, wanted to shelter him from the outside world. The only life they wanted him to know was one of beautiful clothes, rich food, and happy, restful days.

He grew up never learning about pain, suffering, or poverty, and he married a beautiful princess who lived with him in the palace grounds.

But Siddhartha grew more and more curious about the outside world. One day, he had his charioteer take him outside the castle, into the town. There, Siddhartha was shocked by what he saw.

First, he saw an old man and he knew that, with age, people became frail.

Then, he saw a sick man, and he knew that any person could be afflicted with disease.

Finally, he saw a dead man, and he knew that we would all one day die.

Seeing all these things made Siddhartha realize how meaningless his life in the palace really was. He took off his fine clothes and left the palace forever, venturing out into the world with nothing.

On his travels, Siddhartha came to a large tree and he sat beneath it for forty-nine days, meditating. After those forty-nine days, he shared everything he'd learned with five people who traveled far and wide, spreading news of a new religion: Buddhism.

The religion talked about nonviolence, compassion, forgiveness, and tolerance. It said that the world is filled with misery and misery is caused by desire. If we could only stop desiring things, we might stop being miserable.

# RICK GENEST

## (BORN 1985)

Rick was always fascinated with body art.
He'd buy bubblegum just so he could get the fake tattoos
that came inside the wrappers.

He was only fifteen when he found out he had a brain tumor. Doctors said there was a chance he might die, which started Rick thinking about death and dark things. He survived the tumor, but his interest in death carried on, and he decided to mix it with his passion for body art.

After getting his first tattoo, a skull and crossbones, Rick became obsessed, and he carried on getting tattoos until the whole of his body was covered.

People started stopping him for photos in the street, amazed by how he looked. Other people said cruel things, but Rick knew you couldn't be yourself without being picked on by someone.

"I didn't do this to be different," he'd explain. "I did this to be me."

When a traveling circus rolled through his town, Rick joined it and they gave him the name Zombie Boy. He performed alongside Lizard Man,

whose tongue was split in two, and Vampire Woman, who had her teeth sharpened to points. It was difficult work, but at least he'd found a place where he fit in.

One day, Rick's friend asked if he wanted to dress up and pose for some photos. Rick agreed and a world-famous fashion designer ended up seeing the photos when they were used in a magazine. Immediately, he flew Rick to Paris, where a new career began for him.

Now Rick's an international model. He's been in Hollywood films, music videos, and had his face put on a doll for kids. Rick isn't made to feel like a freak anymore. He feels like himself and people love him for it.

# KING GEORGE VI

## (1895–1952)

George never expected to be king. His older brother, Edward, was supposed to take the throne when their father died. And Edward did, for a little while, until he fell in love with a woman who he wasn't allowed to marry, so he stepped down, and George was forced to take his place.

Growing up, George was often frightened, often crying, and often sick. He also had a stammer, which made it difficult for him to speak, and because of that he became embarrassed and shy.

The day he found out he was to be king was terrifying. He went to visit his mother, and he wrote in his diary: "When I told her what had happened, I broke down and sobbed uncontrollably."

One of the things he was most worried about was having to talk in front of people. It was an age when the radio was becoming popular, and the royal family would have to use it to communicate with their people.

To try and prepare him, George was sent to see a speech therapist named Lionel Logue. Lionel believed that the only reason George found it difficult to speak in public was because he was so worried about how he sounded. He thought that, if George couldn't hear himself, he wouldn't need to be worried, and he wouldn't stammer. To test his idea, Lionel put headphones on George, loudly played music into them, and gave him a speech to read. George was frustrated because he didn't think it was working. He stormed out.

Later, when he listened to a recording, he found that he wasn't stammering at all.

With Lionel's help, George gave speeches in public, opened Parliament, and announced to the British people that Britain had decided to go to war with Germany. He stayed friends with Lionel for the rest of his life and ended up being one of the best-loved kings that England had ever had.

# JOHN GREEN

## (BORN 1977)

At school, John wore braces, was bullied, and generally got the kind of grades that you try to hide from your parents. What made it worse was how well his brother, Hank, always did.

As he got older, John realized he wanted to write books for young people—books that didn't speak to them like they were babies. From working at a children's hospital, he knew that young people know and wonder as much as adults about life and death, and they want to read books about those things, too.

After becoming a writer, John started to miss being around people. Because he hardly saw Hank anymore, he suggested that, for an entire year, the two of them communicate with each other through YouTube videos. His brother agreed.

In the videos, they talked about themselves, their lives, science, pizza, giraffes, and Harry Potter. Millions of young people started watching. Through forums and comment sections, the young people became friends and they gave themselves a name: nerdfighters.

The nerdfighters collected money for charity, raised awareness of causes, and tried their best to look out for each other.

One nerdfighter, a warm and hilarious girl named Esther, was sick with cancer when John became friends with her. After she died, he wrote a book inspired by her life: *The Fault in Our Stars*. With the help of the nerdfighters, who spread word of it everywhere they could, the book went on to be a huge bestseller and a hit film.

John and his brother are very close now. Once a year, they tell each other, "I love you." They say it on Esther's birthday, a day celebrated by nerdfighters across the world.

# ALAN L. HART

## (1890–1962)

When he was young, Alan was known as Lucille; his parents named him that because they thought he was a girl. But Alan didn't feel comfortable in his own body. He didn't feel comfortable because he felt as though he was trapped in a girl's body.

"Can I cut my hair and be a boy?" he'd ask his mom.

She wouldn't listen.

When he had to go to school, Alan was forced to wear girls' clothes. He struggled throughout his years there, and, to cope with his problem, he lost himself in his studies, especially science. That hard work earned him a place at a university, where he met and fell in love with a woman. But when Alan wore the boys' clothes he preferred, she left him.

Struggling, Alan went to visit a psychiatrist named Dr. Gilbert. After a lot of tests and questions, Dr. Gilbert diagnosed Alan as transgender. It meant that the body he was in didn't match how he felt inside. According to Dr. Gilbert, Alan had been born a boy in a girl's body. Dr. Gilbert firmly believed that the opposite could be true, too, where girls were born in the bodies of boys.

Alan just wanted to be accepted for the man he was, and to be allowed to study and practice medicine, so Dr. Gilbert performed an operation on him. Alan became one of the first ever transgender people to have their body changed to match how they felt inside.

As well as studying medicine, Alan channeled all of his experiences into novels that became bestsellers. He fell in love with a woman, married her, and they lived together happily for thirty-seven years. During that time, he conducted groundbreaking work on a disease called tuberculosis, and saved a lot of lives.

Society made life difficult for people like Alan, but that never stopped Alan from doing everything he could for society.

# ACHMAT HASSIEM

## (BORN 1982)

One quiet Sunday morning in Cape Town, Achmat and his brother, Tariq, were at the beach practicing with friends for their lifeguard exams. In the exam, some people would pretend to be drowning while the others launched a boat to save them. Tariq swam out and floated, while Achmat stayed near the shore, both waiting to be rescued.

That was when Achmat saw a huge, dark shape barrelling toward his brother. He wasn't sure what it was until a black fin broke the water. The shape was a great white shark.

Trying to distract it, Achmat madly splashed and shouted. His tactic worked. The shark turned and headed for him instead, letting the lifeboat pull Tariq to safety.

But there was no time for the boat to reach Achmat. The shark reared up, its jaw locked open, showing rows and rows of bloody, jagged teeth. Achmat tried to get away. He couldn't move. Looking down, he realized the shark had his entire leg in its mouth.

At the last moment, his brother's hand appeared from above, dragging him aboard the boat.

When he woke up in the hospital, Achmat fell into a depression. His leg was gone. He'd always loved sports and swimming, and now he was worried he wouldn't be able to do either.

Then he got a visit from an athlete named Natalie du Toit. She'd lost her leg when she was seventeen and had become a Paralympic swimmer, winning medals at three different Paralympics. She told him he should try it. He did, and he ended up winning in the Paralympics, too.

As he walked out for the final race, the audience chanted, "Shark boy! Shark boy! Shark boy!"

# STEPHEN HAWKING

## (1942–2018)

School bored Stephen, so he was thrilled when it finished and he could move to the University of Cambridge to learn about cosmology, the study of everything to do with our universe.

Stephen had a lot of big questions. How did the universe start? And why? What came before it? And what exactly are black holes?

He had a special mind, and his work quickly impressed everyone.

Then, when Stephen was twenty-one, his friends and family started to notice that he would trip over and sometimes lose control of his words. They were worried. They sent him to a doctor, who diagnosed him with a disease called ALS, which meant that Stephen's body was slowly shutting down. The doctors said that he only had two more years to live. Hearing that, Stephen threw himself straight back into his investigation of the cosmos.

Stephen lived for more than fifty years past that diagnosis and he is one of the most important physicists to have ever lived. Even though he was in a wheelchair and needed a computer to speak, Stephen never stopped searching for a theory of everything: one single idea that could explain the entire universe and everything in it.

He also found time to write a famous book titled *A Brief History of Time*, which, for a lot of people everywhere, was their first glimpse into the grand mysteries of time and space.

Stephen spent his final years with his children and grandchildren, continuing his research, and traveling to give lectures on the cosmos.

"However difficult life may seem," he says, "there is always something you can do and succeed at. It matters that you don't just give up."

# JIM HENSON

## (1936–1990)

Jim and his best friend, Kermit, used to spend whole days
having adventures and collecting animals out in the woods.
He'd bring them home, too. His grandma always had
to check her chair before she sat down in case he'd
left a turtle or a frog on it.

Out of everyone he knew, Jim was closest to his grandma. She made quilts and did needlework, which she showed to Jim, encouraging him to start work on his own projects.

"What do you want to do most in the world?" she asked him.

Jim thought long and hard. "Puppets," he told her. "I want to make puppets."

"Then do it."

Jim had his own approach to puppetry. Most of the puppets at the time were stiff and made out of wood, but Jim made his out of flexible things, like cloth and rubber, so he could give them more life and expression, like the real creatures he'd seen.

He made his first puppet out of his mom's old coat, a piece of cardboard, and two ping-pong balls. The puppet was a frog called Kermit, named after his old friend.

Then Jim went everywhere looking for a job, and eventually a local TV station hired him to perform with his puppets. They didn't care that he was still in school. For them, it just meant they could pay him less.

The show was canceled after two episodes, but Jim impressed everyone so much that he was invited to try again on an even bigger channel.

Along with his friends Miss Piggy, Fozzie Bear, Gonzo, and all the other Muppets, Kermit starred in TV shows and films and became one of the best-loved characters in the world. These films are still shown in hundreds of countries today. Kermit gave this advice to all the children watching *The Muppet Show*: "Just because you haven't found your talent yet doesn't mean you don't have one."

# RYAN HRELJAC

## (BORN 1991)

One day, when Ryan was six years old, his teacher taught a lesson about Africa. She explained that in some parts of Africa it was almost impossible for people to get clean water. Without clean water, people, and especially children, could get sick and die.

Ryan was shocked. All he had to do was walk into his kitchen and turn on the tap if he wanted something to drink.

He knew he had to help.

After some research, Ryan found an organization called WaterCan that could help African families by digging deep wells and then using pumps to pull clean water from underground. But the wells were expensive to build. So Ryan started doing more chores around the house and saving all his allowance. But it still wasn't enough. He had to think bigger.

He spoke out in public, collected money at school, and did everything he could to fundraise. Eventually, he had enough for a well.

Ryan didn't stop there. He started his own charity, kept raising money, and traveled across the world meeting celebrities, donors, and the children he'd always wanted to help.

His charity, Ryan's Well Foundation, is over eighteen years old now. And it's helped nine hundred thousand people in Africa get clean water.

Someone once asked Ryan what he'd learned. Ryan said he'd learned that the world is like a great big puzzle, with everyone just trying to figure out where they fit in. "I figure my piece fits with clean water," he said. "I just hope everyone else finds out where their puzzle pieces fit, too."

# STEVE IRWIN

## (1962–2006)

As well as two sisters, Steve grew up surrounded by crocodiles, snakes, lizards, koalas, and a host of other animals. His parents ran a wildlife park. Luckily, Steve turned out to love animals as deeply as they did. He was given a pet python for his sixth birthday. By the time he was nine, Steve was out catching crocodiles with his dad.

When he grew up, Steve carried on his work trapping crocodiles that had wandered too close to towns and bringing them back to the park, where they could live undisturbed.

He was so keen on them that, instead of flying out to a peaceful beach on his honeymoon, he and his wife went into the wilderness instead. They spent their days searching for animals and filming their adventures. When a TV channel saw their videos, they asked Steve to make an entire series. They called it *The Crocodile Hunter*.

In the show, Steve and his wife introduced the Australian public to all kinds of strange and deadly creatures, from snakes to spiders, and birds to beetles.

"By crikey!" he would shout, staring into the jaws of a giant alligator. "Look at this beauty!"

Every year, he put one million dollars into a charity that bought areas of land in Australia and tried to return them to their natural state. His real passion was conservation. Even though his shows were entertaining, the point of them was to draw people's attention to the animals.

He didn't want people to think of certain animals as scary or dangerous. He wanted people to know they were beautiful creatures that we have a responsibility to look after, not just for their sake, but for ours, too.

Sadly, Steve died in 2006, while he was out shooting a documentary about stingrays.

His father said he wouldn't have had it any other way.

# JAMES EARL JONES

## (BORN 1931)

Even though you might not know his name, you'd definitely recognize James Earl Jones's voice. James has been the voice of Darth Vader in *Star Wars*, Mufasa in *The Lion King*, the Giant in *Jack and the Beanstalk*, as well as countless others. But he wasn't always such a confident speaker.

From the age of five, James was raised by his grandparents. Life with them was so difficult that James developed a severe stutter and refused to speak because of it. For eight years, he remained almost completely silent. It wasn't until an English teacher discovered his gift for poetry that James started speaking.

"It's too good for you to have written," the teacher told him, after reading one of his poems. "So please stand up and recite it from memory to prove that you did."

James did it without stuttering. He'd found his voice again.

He went to college to study medicine, but soon realized that acting was where his heart was, so he switched courses. While he was studying, he also met his father for the first time in his life, and his father encouraged him to devote his attention to acting. They lived together, polishing theater floors for money, while James auditioned for parts in plays.

For a long time, he carried a spear in the New York Shakespeare Festival's production of *Henry V*. His parts got bigger after that, appearing on the big screen in films such as *Conan the Barbarian* and *Field of Dreams*, as well as on the stage in productions like *Hamlet* and *Fences*. James has played a huge number of different characters.

He once said, "One of the hardest things in life is having words in your heart that you can't utter." James is living proof that even when it feels impossible, we shouldn't give up on finding our voices.

# CHIEF JOSEPH

## (1840–1904)

Chief Joseph's real name was Hin-mah-too-yah-lat-kekt, which means "thunder rolling down the mountain" in English. He was the leader of a band of Native Americans who belonged to the Nez Perce tribe and lived in the Wallowa Valley.

When people arrived from across the ocean, carrying guns and swords, the Native Americans were forced off the land on which they'd lived peacefully for thousands of years.

When gold was found on Nez Perce land, they were told they would have to move to a reservation. Reservations were small areas of land where the Native Americans were sent so that the settlers could use their lands for themselves.

The government told the tribe that they had thirty days to leave or there would be a war.

Most of the other leaders were in favor of fighting. They didn't want to leave behind their ancestors, their homes, and everything they'd ever known. Chief Joseph said he would rather say good-bye than fight.

So his band of Nez Perce began their long and dangerous ride north to Canada. They hoped to meet up with Chief Sitting Bull and his tribe, who'd fled in that direction after a vicious, bloody war.

For the three months they traveled, they were chased and attacked by the settlers. Through skill and intelligence, they managed to beat and escape their pursuers, even though the settlers' weapons were better and their numbers were bigger.

After a five-day battle in freezing weather, just a few miles from the Canadian border, Chief Joseph was forced to surrender. He told his people, "I am tired. My heart is sick and sad. From where the sun now stands, I will fight no more forever."

The Nez Perce were sent to live on reservations. Chief Joseph spent the rest of his life campaigning for the Native Americans to be allowed back to their homelands. He never let the world forget how his people had been treated.

# WILLIAM KAMKWAMBA

## (BORN 1987)

William was born in a small village in Malawi,
where the houses are thatched and built from mud bricks,
and tall golden grasses surround them like fences.

For William to go to school, his parents had to pay eighty dollars every year. They were farmers, like a lot of people in Malawi. They ate most of what they grew and sold whatever was left over to raise money. One year, there was a famine, so the Kamkwambas couldn't earn any money and William couldn't go to school.

Even though there was no one to teach him, William decided he could teach himself. He went to the nearest library and started reading.

Electronics interested him most. From books, he learned how to repair radios, and he set up his own business repairing the radios of the people in his village.

Then he found a book called *Using Energy*, which spoke about how wind turbines could create electricity by harnessing the power of the wind. Using trees, an old fan, and a broken bicycle, William managed to build his own wind turbine to power his house.

Everyone who saw it was amazed. When journalists heard William's story, it became news all over the world, and he was invited to give talks and go on trips abroad. Different people offered to pay for William to start his education again, and money also came in for him to work on other projects around his village. Since the first windmill, he's created more turbines, solar power, clean water, and soccer uniforms and equipment for his village team.

# JOHN LENNON

## (1940–1980)

In the 1960s, war was raging in Vietnam; the north and the south were locked in a fierce battle and each side had powerful allies in other countries. Millions of young Americans had signed up to fight. As they crawled through the dank and unfamiliar mud of the jungle, planes dropped bombs through the trees overhead.

Life was very different for John. He'd been in a band named the Beatles, one of the most famous bands ever to exist, and they'd just broken up. Free of the band, he could finally do what he wanted to do: try to move the world toward peace by putting a stop to the Vietnam War.

The first thing he did was marry his girlfriend, Yoko Ono. The second thing they did together was go on honeymoon. They didn't go to a beautiful beach on an island; they went to a hotel in Amsterdam, got into bed, and stayed there for two weeks. Every day, they invited journalists into their hotel room and they would talk to them about peace and love.

They wanted to let young people know that there are a lot of ways to protest the things that you don't agree with. If it's peaceful, protest can be anything: growing your hair, giving up your vacation, or sitting still until you're heard.

John also fought for peace with his music, like his song "Give Peace a Chance."

In 1969, when half a million people marched through the streets of Washington in protest, that is the song they sang.

Each protester held a sign showing the name of a dead American soldier or a village in Vietnam that had been destroyed. The fighting went on for another six years and over a million lives were lost.

Unfortunately, John's life ended early when he was shot. But he wasn't forgotten. Every year, on New Year's Eve, his song "Imagine" is played in the center of New York City. "You may say I'm a dreamer," he sings. "But I'm not the only one."

# CARL LINNAEUS

## (1707–1778)

*Bufo bufo* means "toad." We are *Homo sapiens*.
And *Argentinosaurus huinculensis* is the name
of a dinosaur that was as heavy as an airplane.

The reason scientists use this way of naming living things is all thanks to a man named Carl Linnaeus, who was born in Sweden in 1707.

Even when he was little, Carl was obsessed with plants. He wanted to know the names of them all and he spent every second of his time in the garden. People thought he was strange.

At school, he was more interested in nature than anything else, so his teacher suggested he study medicine, which he did.

One warm summer afternoon, his university professor found him wandering between flowers in the scientific garden. Curious, the professor decided to test him.

"What's this?" he asked, pointing to a shrub with pink leaves.

"Honeysuckle," Carl told him straight away. "Native to Siberia and East Asia. Don't eat the fruit; it's poisonous, and you might die."

The professor was amazed. He tried another—Carl knew it. And another—Carl knew that, too. The professor was so impressed that he gave Carl a place to live, a library to use, and made him a teacher at the university.

It was then that Carl worked hard to spread news of a new way of naming things: the binomial system. In the system, every living thing on Earth has a two-word name. Because of this system, scientists across the planet, speaking in different languages, would know when they were speaking about the same plant or creature. Carl named over twelve thousand species himself. He also made it a lot easier for us to make sense of the magnificent world of nature.

# NELSON MANDELA

## (1918–2013)

In the 1600s and 1700s, British and Dutch colonists arrived in South Africa and took power, resources, and land away from the native black South Africans. By 1948, white people had control of the government. They didn't let black South Africans vote, interact with white people, or even move out of the areas in which they lived.

Nelson, whose name actually means "troublemaker" in one South African language, was born in a small village in 1918. He was appalled by the treatment of his people and began joining groups to fight against it. For doing so, he was kicked out of college.

Next, he joined a group called the African National Congress, and campaigned with them.

The government declared him a terrorist. They arrested him, found him guilty of treason, and threw him in jail. His enemies called for him to be executed. But the judge gave him a life sentence instead.

Nelson was so well known for his activism that, while he was in jail, the rest of the world began to look at how black people were being treated in

South Africa. They put pressure on the white government to release him. Eventually, many years later, the white president Frederik de Klerk did.

"If you want to make peace with your enemy," Nelson said, "you have to work with your enemy."

And that is what he did. With Frederik, Nelson wrote new laws that would give South Africans of all colors the same rights.

By 1994, Nelson had gone from spending twenty-seven years in prison to being his country's first democratically elected president. All that time, he'd never given up hope.

# WILLIAM MOULTON MARSTON

## (1893–1947)

In the 1940s, comic books and the superheroes who inhabited them became really popular. There were hundreds of them, like Batman and Superman and Flash and the Green Lantern.

But there weren't any girls.

It made no sense.

Girls read comics, too, but they never got to see themselves in them. Not as superheroes, at least. All women in comic books seemed to do was get kidnapped and then get rescued by men.

One night, William Moulton Marston was explaining to his wife, Elizabeth, an idea he'd had for a new kind of superhero. This new superhero, he said, wouldn't rely on a weapon or fighting, but on being clever and being kind.

"Fine," his wife said. "Just make her a woman."

And Wonder Woman was born.

William was a Harvard psychology professor who spent a lot of his time being fired from jobs for speaking up for women. During his studies, he'd become increasingly interested in women's rights, and he based Wonder Woman's character on early feminists and suffragettes—strong, powerful women who were capable of rescuing themselves.

In the comics, Wonder Woman comes from a lost world called Paradise Island, where women live peacefully without men. Then, one day, a man crash-lands on the island and Wonder Woman has to take him home. Back in his land, she finds herself caught up in a series of adventures, taking down evil gods and villains.

To help her, she has superhuman strength, bracelets that deflect bullets, and a lasso that can get the truth out of anyone.

She was a hit, with girls and boys, and new stories about her haven't stopped being released since.

# IQBAL MASIH

## (1983–1995)

At the age of four, Iqbal started work at a carpet factory in Pakistan. When his mom got sick, she borrowed one hundred dollars from the owner of the factory to have an operation. She couldn't pay the money back. Instead, she had to give Iqbal to the factory owner as a slave.

There, he was forced to work long hours in a tiny, hot space filled with noisy and dangerous equipment. He had to work relentlessly and was beaten if he ever slowed down.

When Iqbal was ten, he escaped. He ran to the police and explained everything. Instead of helping, the police took him back to the factory and claimed a reward. This time, Iqbal was chained to the carpet machine so he couldn't get away.

One day, he spotted a poster for an organization called the Bonded Labor Liberation Front, who aimed to rescue people from captivity. He secretly contacted them. They told him that slavery had been ended and all slaves were supposed to have been released.

With the help of the BLLF, Iqbal and some of the other children from his factory were allowed to leave. But it wasn't happening everywhere. Most factory owners were ignoring the new laws and keeping children trapped in their factories, chained to the clanking machines.

Iqbal made it his mission to set them free.

He snuck into factories and told the kids trapped there about their rights. He spoke at meetings and rallies, to businesses and factory owners, on behalf of the enslaved children. He was even flown around the world to talk about his plight and the plight of others like him.

In 1995, Iqbal was murdered for speaking out against the factory owners. By that time, he'd helped save the lives of over three thousand trapped children who felt as though they'd been forgotten.

# DON McPHERSON

## (BORN 1965)

Don McPherson was a famous American football player, but he never really felt comfortable playing sports. He didn't like how competitive it was. He didn't like how tough everyone acted. And he especially didn't like how people treated each other.

A lot of things didn't make sense to him.

Why do we look up to people just because they can throw or kick a ball? Why are we so aggressive when we play? Is that a good way to act? And why do men insult each other by saying, "You throw like a girl?" Why would you talk about women being less able? What does that say about you?

Instead of playing football, Don now travels the country, talking to young people about masculinity, feminism, and sports. Especially in sports, he thinks that men often think and talk about women in negative ways, and that thinking and talking has

consequences. Girls often stop playing sports at school because they've lost their confidence. Right now, all across the world, women are feeling unsafe because of how they're treated by men.

Don believes that the way to end this isn't just to treat women better ourselves, but to stand up and say something when we see people who aren't.

"You can do this," he says. "We can do this. Together, men and women can build a safer world."

# CHRISTIAN McPHILAMY

Children can lose their hair for many reasons.
It can happen because they're being treated for cancer,
or have been burned, or can't stop themselves from pulling
it out. Not having hair can mean they get bullied and
end up losing all their confidence.

Christian was six years old when he saw a commercial on TV explaining all that. He knew he wanted to help, and he decided that the best way to do it would be to grow his hair and then donate it, so it could be made into a wig for a child who needed it more than he did.

For two years, Christian stopped getting haircuts. His hair grew longer and longer and became a bright blonde mane that hung down to his waist.

Sometimes, classmates, coaches, or friends of his parents would tell him to cut it off and even offer him money to do it. They said he looked like a girl. Christian didn't care and he wasn't going to cut it. He made sure he took the time to explain to whoever was criticizing or making fun of him exactly what he was doing and why he was doing it. When they found out that he was trying to help sick kids, a lot of people felt embarrassed and apologized.

Two years after he first saw the commercial, he felt ready. Christian's family gathered around him and shaved off all his hair. Altogether, he'd managed to grow four ponytails that were each as long as ten caterpillars. The hair was sent away to the Children With Hair Loss charity, and Christian made life a lot happier for several young boys and girls.

# LIONEL MESSI

## (BORN 1987)

Lionel Messi was eleven when he was diagnosed
with a condition called growth hormone deficiency.
The condition meant that his body wasn't growing as fast
as it should. To treat it, he needed expensive medicine,
but his dad worked in a factory and his mom was a janitor,
so they couldn't afford it.

Even at that age, Messi showed amazing talent as a soccer player, and a team in his country, Argentina, wanted to sign him. But the team couldn't pay for his medicine, so he had to turn them down.

Next, Messi tried out for the Barcelona team, where he impressed the coach so much that they agreed to pay for his treatment. The coach was in such a hurry to sign him and get him healthy, he wrote the contract on the nearest piece of paper: a napkin from the restaurant they were eating in.

Very quickly, Messi proved himself to be one of the greatest soccer players in history.

In 2012, he broke the record for the most goals scored in a year. The previous record was eighty-five and

had stood for forty years. That year, Messi scored ninety-one.

When he was asked to move to the English Premier League, he said no. When he was offered more money than any soccer player ever, to join a Russian team, Messi said no to that, too. He still felt loyal to Barcelona, who'd helped him as a child when he needed it most.

And because he knows how it feels to need help, he now campaigns for the rights of children, runs his own charity, and donates money to hospitals so they can afford to care for young people who need it.

# HARVEY MILK
## (1930–1978)

Harvey realized he was gay when he was fourteen, but at first he chose not to tell anyone. After school, he joined the navy. Later, he fell in love and moved with his partner to San Francisco, where they opened a camera shop. While working there, Harvey discovered how much he enjoyed helping people with their problems, perhaps because he hadn't let anyone help him when he needed it most. To carry on helping others, he decided to go into politics.

He wanted to gain a position on the city council. In the first election, he came in tenth. In the second, seventh. In the third, fourth. And then, finally, Harvey succeeded, becoming the first openly gay elected official in the history of the city.

Straight away, he got to work. He created programs for minorities, workers, and the elderly. He passed a law that made it illegal for employers or landlords to discriminate based on sexuality. He promoted free public transportation and affordable childcare. He even made it illegal not to clear up your dog's poo.

When a law was put forward that would have prevented gay and lesbian teachers from working in schools in California, he put a stop to that.

On November 27, 1978, an angry, troubled man, who opposed what Harvey stood for, shot and killed him in his office.

The whole city was distraught.

Thirty thousand people marched with candles to show how much Harvey had meant to them. He became a symbol for the whole gay-rights movement. In 2009, Barack Obama awarded him the Presidential Medal of Freedom, and every year, on May 22, people across America celebrate Harvey Milk Day.

# CAINE MONROY

## (BORN 2002)

In Los Angeles, school had finished for the summer, and Caine was spending his days at the auto shop where his dad worked. He was nine years old and there wasn't a lot to do.

To fill time, Caine started building an arcade. He'd always loved arcades, and now he wanted his own. He built it from the cardboard boxes that stock for the shop arrived in. With scissors and tape, he made machines, stands for prizes, a security system, and even uniforms.

Caine dreamed of his arcade filling with people. He would offer them four turns for a dollar, or two dollars for a Fun Pass, which would get them five hundred turns. The prizes they'd get for winning would be his toys.

No customers came. But Caine wouldn't shut down his arcade.

On the last day of summer, a filmmaker named Nirvan Mullick came in to buy a new handle for his car. Before he left, he ended up buying a Fun Pass. Nirvan was so entranced by the arcade that he wanted to make a film of it, and of Caine, to let the world know what Caine had been doing.

When the video went online, it was watched over a million times in the first day.

Nirvan wanted to use the attention to help Caine. He set up a fund to raise money so that Caine could eventually afford to go to college, and the fund made over $200,000.

Together, Nirvan and Caine created a website called Imagination.org, which aims to inspire creativity in schools, homes, and communities everywhere. Their mission is to get kids using their imaginations to change the world for the better. By setting challenges and sharing stories, the site has encouraged over a million young people to think creatively and have a lot of fun while doing so.

# JORGE MUÑOZ

## (BORN 1964)

For over twenty years, Jorge drove children to and from school in New York City. His family was from Colombia, but his mom, Doris, had taken him and his sister, Luz, to America, looking for a new life after their father was killed in an accident.

One day, after dropping off his bus full of children at school, Jorge spoke with a group of men standing underneath a bridge. The men were immigrants from other countries, just like Jorge. They explained to him that they stood under the bridge every day, shivering in thunderstorms and sweating in heat waves, waiting to be chosen for small jobs so they could make money to send home to their families. They told him they were so poor that they sometimes went days without eating anything at all.

The next day, when Jorge was getting ready for work, he packed eight extra lunches; he then handed them out to workers waiting under the bridge.

Some days after that, he passed a food factory at closing time and saw that they were throwing out perfectly good leftovers. He asked the factory workers if he could use them to feed the immigrant workers. The workers said yes.

With his mom and sister, Jorge bought a freezer so big it filled their living room. Every day, before and after work, the family cooks and hands out hot meals for workers. Most of the money comes from Jorge's paycheck as a bus driver.

Since it all began, Jorge and his family have served over 100,000 meals to people in need. They know how it feels to be hungry and homesick in a new country. Some of the people under that bridge may be poor, homeless, and missing their families, but at least they can count on a good, hot meal, thanks to the generosity of Jorge.

# TREVOR NOAH

## (BORN 1984)

Trevor says he was born a crime. His dad is white, his mom is black, and he comes from South Africa, where any mixing between the two was illegal.

When his mom was caught in his dad's building, she was put in jail. If they were outside together, his mom wasn't allowed to hold his dad's hand, and his dad would have to walk on the other side of the road.

So Trevor was raised by his grandmother and his mother, until his mom married a violent man who terrified Trevor and once shot his mom in the head. Somehow, she survived, and she continued looking after Trevor as best she could.

School was hard, too, because he felt like he couldn't fit in with the white kids or the black kids. Trevor also suffered from a lot of painful spots and had to take medicine to get them under control, which had side effects, like making him tired and unhappy.

His family was so poor they would eat worms. To start the car, they'd roll it down the hill to save petrol. To make money, he played DJ sets in the streets with his friends.

As he grew up, Trevor decided to make use of everything he'd been through. He wanted to put his experiences into comedy. Even when he talked about the saddest, most difficult times of his life, he managed to find the funny side. And he took his comedy all over South Africa, sharing his pain and laughter with strangers.

Trevor's since moved to America.

He hosts the biggest American comedy news show and is a famous stand-up comedian. He says he owes it all to his mom's determination that he would get out of poverty.

"In my world," he said, "a woman was the most powerful thing that I knew. Still is."

# TENZING NORGAY

## (1914–1986)

At 11:30 a.m. on May 29, 1953, Tenzing Norgay and Edmund Hillary became the first people in history to reach the top of the world's tallest mountain, Mount Everest. Above the clouds, surrounded by gigantic glaciers and thrashed by strong winds, Edmund solemnly stuck out his hand for a traditional handshake. Tenzing was so excited, he ignored the hand and dragged Edmund in for a big hug instead.

Edmund was an explorer from New Zealand who'd had a very privileged upbringing. But Tenzing had started off with nothing in his life. He had been born in the mountains and sold into slavery as a boy. He'd never learned to read. He didn't even know when his own birthday was.

Tenzing ran away while he was being forced to work for a rich family, and he reached India, where he fell in love and got married.

At nineteen, he was chosen to help with his first expedition up Everest. He did so well that whenever other groups from around the world came to try and reach the summit, they would always ask him to help. He knew the mountains better than they did, could carry more than anyone else, and was a lot more used to the ropes, lines, and tents.

Tenzing helped on many expeditions before attempting the climb with Edmund. After they'd reached the top of Everest together, both became celebrities. It meant Tenzing could afford to buy a house for his family, set up his own adventuring company, and send his kids to universities in America, where they'd get the kind of education he'd never had.

Since he'd never known his birthday, he decided to give himself one, and he chose May 29: the day he'd reached the top of the world's tallest mountain.

# RIC O'BARRY

## (BORN 1939)

Dolphins play catch with each other for fun, use tools to find food, and communicate in their own language. Some people think they're almost as intelligent as humans.

Ric used to work for a sea-life center, capturing and training dolphins for entertainment. The dolphins were made to perform on TV and in live shows, where they'd have to jump through hoops, spin through the air, and wave their fins at loud crowds. It was an exciting and glamorous life for Ric. Celebrities often came to visit and he was earning a lot of money.

One day, one of the dolphins Ric was working with died. It was far younger than it should have been. He knew that the dolphin wouldn't have died in the wild, and it made him so upset that he quit his job, deciding to devote his life to freeing these intelligent creatures instead.

With a friend, he created the Dolphin Project. Its aim is to learn as much as possible about dolphins, as well as to untrain those in sea-life centers and public aquariums, so they can be released back into the wild. In captivity, baby dolphins are often born in cramped glass tanks, where they'll never know how it feels to leap in the ocean, chase ships, and hunt for their own food. All they know is boredom and how to perform for humans, so without the help of Ric and his team, they'd never be able to survive once they're released into their natural environment.

"In a world where so much that is wild and free has been lost to us," he says, "we must leave these beautiful animals free to swim as they will and must."

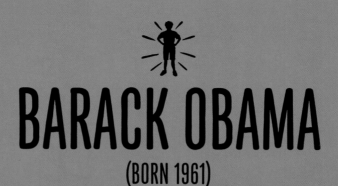

# BARACK OBAMA

## (BORN 1961)

A lot of people said that the United States of America would never have a black president. But all of those people were wrong.

In 1961, Barack Obama was born in Honolulu, an American island in the Pacific Ocean. He was six when he moved to Indonesia, a place where people ate snakes and grasshoppers and the kids battled with kites in the street. Some years, there was no rain and people went hungry. Other years, there was so much rain that it rushed along the roads in rivers.

It was a difficult place to live, and eventually Barack was sent back to America.

He grew up, married a woman named Michelle, and had two daughters, Sasha and Malia.

But his country wasn't doing as well. The American economy was in trouble, which meant people were poorer than they'd been in a long time and there weren't enough jobs to go around. Americans wanted change. Wanting to help, Barack ran for president. Despite hundreds of years of racism, despite racist attacks from competitors, and

despite it having been only fifty years since black people were allowed to vote, the American people elected Barack as president.

He didn't seem like any president that had come before him. He collected Spider-Man comics and played basketball and even danced on TV shows.

He also created millions of new jobs, helped poorer people get medicine, ended two wars, and made it illegal to treat gay people or women differently than anyone else.

And he did all that while raising his daughters alongside his wife. For Malia and Sasha, he was just trying to help create a world where everyone had a chance to be whoever they wanted to be.

"That's what twenty-first century feminism is about," he said, "the idea that when everyone is equal, we are all more free."

# FRANK OCEAN
## (BORN 1987)

All Frank wanted to be when he grew up was a singer. As a teenager, he would mow people's lawns, wash their cars, and walk their dogs to raise money so that he could get into a studio and record his songs. He lived in New Orleans, Louisiana.

One day, a huge hurricane tore through the city. Thousands of people lost their lives, their homes, and everything they had. The studios where Frank had recorded his songs were gone, too.

So he moved to Los Angeles to keep making music. He worked nonstop. And to support himself, he got jobs making sandwiches and typing boring lists of numbers into computers. Finally, he got a songwriting contract; every day, he went to the studio and wrote hip-hop, rap, and pop songs for other people who needed songs written for them.

Eventually, he started releasing his own music and people were amazed.

He signed a record deal. He recorded his first album.

The night before it came out, Frank wrote a letter to his fans, telling the story of a long summer night when he'd first fallen in love and how the person he'd fallen in love with had been a man.

People asked if he was gay. He told them labels didn't matter to him.

"I feel like a free man," he said. "If I listen closely, I can hear the sky falling, too."

Other musicians wrote messages of support, talking about how courageous he was. It was courageous because, for a long time, it felt like the hip-hop community wouldn't be tolerant of gay people.

Frank doesn't like being famous, but he's grateful. He sometimes wishes he'd worn a mask so no one would know what he looks like. After his album did so well, he escaped his record label, disappeared, and didn't reappear for years. Everyone had to wait four years for Frank to release his new album because he wanted it to be perfect. When it did finally come out, they loved him more than ever. He'd made something that was true to himself.

# CHRISTOPHER PAOLINI

## (BORN 1983)

Christopher didn't like to read before his mom dragged him to the library. He hadn't wanted to learn how and didn't think he'd ever find reading useful. But on that trip, he picked up a book that led him into another world, and since then he's never wanted to come home.

After one particular story, Christopher started seeing great swooping dragons everywhere. He saw them in the shower, in the garden, and even when he closed his eyes.

He knew it had to mean something.

It meant he had to write.

Using knowledge he'd gained from camping in the mountains behind his house, building shelters, making swords, tracking animals, and practicing archery, Christopher began work on an epic fantasy novel set in a land that came straight from his own imagination. He was fifteen. One year later, he'd finished the book.

The book was titled *Eragon*. It told the story of a farm boy who finds a dragon egg and is forced to flee his hometown when an evil king comes looking for it.

At first, Christopher published the book with the help of his parents. He even drew the cover himself. To promote it, he went around different schools for a whole year, dressed in medieval costume, and read parts of his story.

Eventually, an editor for a big publisher heard about him, read the book, and published it around the world. It was an instant bestseller.

In 2011, Guinness World Records recognized him as the Youngest Author of a Bestselling Book Series.

# SERGEI POLUNIN

## (BORN 1989)

Even as a ten-year-old, Sergei could spin through the air, fly like he was on strings, and bend as though he was made of clay.

He grew up in a small town in the Ukraine. It was so small, his mom said that the only choice he had there was which type of cabbage to have for dinner. If he wanted to make something of himself, he'd have to go somewhere else.

But his family was poor and it would be expensive to move. To raise the money, his dad left to work in Portugal and sent money back so that Sergei and his mom could move to a bigger town where Sergei could study dance.

It got hard being apart and his parents divorced.

When he was thirteen, Sergei earned a place at the Royal Ballet School in London, and he moved there to study ballet. By the time he was nineteen, he'd become the youngest main dancer ever in the Royal Ballet. He won awards and medals, and people said he might be the best dancer alive.

None of it made Sergei happy.

Sergei always thought that, by earning money from dancing, he'd be able to bring his family back together. He couldn't. And he didn't want to do it anymore.

So he left. Right in the middle of a rehearsal. And never came back.

The next time he appeared was in a music video for a rock song. In the video, Sergei dances alone in an abandoned old barn. The video's been watched over eighteen million times.

Now, he puts together his own dances and shows with his own dancers and friends. He prefers to do things his own way.

# DANIEL RADCLIFFE

## (BORN 1989)

At school, Daniel never really felt he was good at anything. He had a problem called dyspraxia, which made even little things, like writing or tying his laces, more difficult for him than for other people. He didn't have much confidence in himself.

Despite that, Daniel always knew he wanted to act. But it was almost an accident when he went to audition to play Harry Potter, the boy wizard who millions of readers everywhere had fallen in love with. Daniel had wanted to give up acting completely when he was eleven. It was only because they couldn't find the right boy anywhere that the director persuaded him to audition.

As soon as he walked into the room, everyone working on the film agreed: this boy must play Harry Potter.

And, for the next ten years, he did. He went to Hogwarts School of Witchcraft and Wizardry, played quidditch, flew on a hippogriff, battled a giant snake, and ultimately defeated Lord Voldemort. As Harry grew up, so did Daniel. Both he and his character shared the same burdens of being recognized wherever they went, being subject to great expectations, and even being bullied at school.

Daniel's glad that he took the part in *Harry Potter*, not because it made him famous or rich, but because it meant he hadn't let the dyspraxia stop him from doing anything he wanted to. And now he has the chance to do good for others.

To help, he has supported the United Kingdom-based charity Get Connected, now known as The Mix, which is a service for young people in need of advice. Instead of buying him Christmas presents, he once asked fans to send money to a hospital for sick children. And, in the United States, he's worked with The Trevor Project, a phone line that young LGBTQ people can call if they feel sad, alone, or unsafe.

"Some people think I'm gay," he said. "Which I think is awesome."

# GHYSLAIN RAZA

Ghyslain loved Star Wars. He loved the sleek spaceships, laser battles fought through space, and the grand struggle between Good and Evil. He loved it so much that he recorded a video of himself swinging a golf stick like a Jedi with a lightsaber.

Unfortunately, some boys at his school found the video. They uploaded it to the Internet without asking him first. Overnight, millions of people had watched Ghyslain playing around at being a Jedi. And they weren't kind about it in their comments.

The worst part for Ghyslain was coming across these comments when he read about his video online. People he didn't even know were making fun of him. At school, he was bullied so badly that he had to leave. He wasn't safe on the streets either. He never knew when he'd be recognized and laughed or shouted at. He felt worthless and alone.

He had become famous for all the wrong reasons. Reporters wouldn't stop calling his house. Ghyslain was invited for TV interviews. Characters in famous cartoons made fun of him.

It took time, but Ghyslain slowly got his confidence back. He went to college and got a degree, and the parents of the boys who'd stolen his video had to pay a lot of money to his family for the pain they'd caused.

Ghyslain wanted to send a message to any kids in similar situations: "You'll survive. You're not alone. You are surrounded by people who love you."

Years later, lots of people proudly post videos online of themselves wielding lightsabers. There's even a group dedicated to teaching lightsaber choreography: the Golden Gate Knights.

"Ghyslain Raza helped blaze a trail for other Star Wars fans," said their leader. "In a way, he was our chosen one that brought us all into the light."

# HANS SCHOLL

## (1918–1943)

When the Nazis took control of Germany,
they killed millions of innocent people and
took freedom away from everyone.

At their university, Hans, his sisters Sophie and Inge, and their friends started held secret talks about the Nazis and how cruel and unfair their actions were.

They decided to create a secret group: the White Rose.

The White Rose printed leaflets that described how the Nazis were killing Jews, disabled people, and other minorities. They talked about nonviolent resistance, the same as Gandhi had practiced. The problem was that a lot of people didn't know what was going on or what they could do about it, and the White Rose wanted to change that.

Their leaflets were posted to schools, bars, cafes, and houses found randomly in the phonebook. Soon, the effects were felt. Anti-Nazi graffiti appeared on the city walls. "Hitler is a murderer!" read one piece. "Down with the Nazis!" cried another.

One day, Hans and his sister, Sophie, were stopped and searched. The police found a draft of a new leaflet in his pocket and knew they'd caught two of the leaders of the White Rose. At the age of twenty-four, Hans was executed for standing up to the Nazis.

But the group's work didn't stop there. One White Rose leaflet was smuggled out of Germany, to England, where thousands of copies were made. English planes flying over German cities dropped the leaflets in the streets, letting the people know what was happening in their country and what they could do to fight it.

Despite fear, despite the possibility of death, and despite living under one of the most terrifying regimes ever to exist, Hans, Sophie, and rest of the White Rose never stopped fighting for what they believed in.

# PERCY SHELLEY

## (1792–1822)

Percy couldn't understand sports, didn't know how to talk to other boys, and spent most of his time buried in books. He was bullied at school. The bullying made him angry, and his anger made the bullying worse. Once, he stabbed another boy with a fork. They called him Mad Shelley, and he felt more alone than he ever had before. It was as though a monster kept taking control of him.

When he moved on to college, Percy met a friend at last. They would stay up late, talking, arguing, and working on projects together. One of their works, a book about how they couldn't believe in God, got them both thrown out of school.

Percy's father was furious. And he was double furious when, instead of applying to other universities, Percy ran away to Scotland with one of his sister's friends. While there, Percy spent his time scribbling down thoughts and poems and sending them out into the world in paper boats, glass bottles, and tiny hot-air balloons.

Then he met a woman named Mary.

They ran away to Paris, and from there they walked all through Europe. As they walked, they read aloud to each other from books. At night, they both wrote. Percy worked on poems that turned out to be some of the most beautiful and important ever written in English. Mary wrote a book called *Frankenstein*, about a grotesque monster and the scientist who'd created him.

Percy made friends with the other great poets of the age, Byron and Keats, and they spent their days together reading, writing, and rowing boats.

# BOYAN SLAT

## (BORN 1994)

On vacation in Greece, sixteen-year-old Boyan dived into the glistening sea, excited to swim among shoals of exotic fish. But Boyan was shocked. He could barely see any fish; all he could really see were plastic bags.
He wanted to know why.

When he got home, Boyan started researching and was surprised by what he found.

Every year, more and more plastic trash is dumped into the earth's oceans. The plastic poisons animals like turtles, seals, and birds, and it can also be swallowed by fish, which humans then go on to eat, making us sick. All of the plastic waste lumps together in vast garbage patches that are impossible for animals to avoid. One of the largest, the Great Pacific Garbage Patch, is twice the size of the United States of America.

Boyan wanted to change that.

He got to work and invented a new type of ocean cleaner that would drift along on the currents, collecting plastic as the seawater passed through it.

Some scientists were doubtful that Boyan's invention would work, but after a whole year of tests, he proved to them that it would. People were so impressed that his company raised over thirty million dollars to start their work.

Within ten years, Ocean Cleanup will have halved the size of the Pacific Garbage Patch. In 2014, Boyan became the youngest person ever to be given the title Champion of the Earth. Hopefully, within his lifetime, he'll be able to leap back into the same Greek sea that started it all and watch thousands of beautiful fish dart through water as clear as glass.

# VEDRAN SMAILOVIĆ

## (BORN 1956)

The city of Sarajevo was being torn to pieces by the war that raged around it. For 1,425 days, tanks rolled through the streets, bombs crashed, and shots were fired. It would be the longest ever siege of a city in the history of modern war.

One afternoon, Vedran heard an explosion and looked out of his window. A bomb had gone off and killed twenty-two people who'd been waiting in line to buy bread at the bakery.

Vedran slumped to the ground.

He felt so angry, so sad, and so powerless. His life, his country, and his friends were all being destroyed, and what could he do about it? He wasn't a soldier, he couldn't fight. He wasn't a politician, he couldn't negotiate. He was a musician. How would that help?

Doing the only thing he could do, Vedran put on his fanciest suit, picked up his cello, and went down into the smoke-filled streets of his city. He set up a stool in the hole left by the bomb and played.

A journalist came to interview him.

"Are you crazy?" the journalist asked.

"You ask me am I crazy for playing the cello?" Vedran replied. "Why do you not ask if they are crazy for destroying Sarajevo?"

He played in the same spot for the next twenty-two days: a day for each person who had died. He played on as buildings burned, bombs fell, and shells flew around him. He played for peace. He played for humanity. And he played to show that, even in the darkest, most terrifying times, there can be hope and beauty, if you only remember to look.

# STEVEN SPIELBERG
## (BORN 1946)

Growing up was difficult for Steven. His family was Jewish, and neighbors and kids at school would shout insults at him because of it.

One night, Steven snuck out of his bedroom and covered all his neighbors' windows in peanut butter. When they confronted his mom, she laughed and told them she was proud of him. But Steven still often felt uncomfortable about being Jewish.

Luckily, he found he could forget about all this when he made films. He loved using his family's home movie camera, making videos of family camping trips and birthday parties. For his first movie, he crashed his toy trains and filmed it. He found he much preferred writing scripts and cutting his films to playing with the other kids in his school.

As he grew up, Steven became famous as a film director. He made films about killer sharks, aliens, dinosaurs, and time travel. But he hadn't ever made a film about being Jewish.

Then he heard the story of Oskar Schindler. During World War II, when the Nazis were killing Jews in great numbers, Oskar saved the lives of over a thousand Jews by giving them jobs in his factories. He spent his entire fortune paying Nazis not to take them away. Steven knew it was a story that needed to be told.

Actually, it was so important, he didn't even think he was good enough to make it, so he asked other people if they'd do it first. When they said no, Steven traveled around Poland to see the places behind the real history.

"Jewish life came pouring back into my heart," he said. "I cried all the time."

Once it was released, the film earned over twenty awards. It's now classed as one of the best films of the past hundred years.

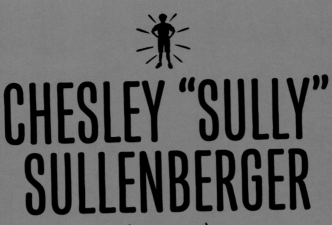

# CHESLEY "SULLY" SULLENBERGER

## (BORN 1951)

Flight 1549 had just taken off from New York's LaGuardia Airport when it struck a huge flock of squawking geese. Both engines cut out. The plane was 3,000 feet in the air and traveling at 250 miles per hour.

Thankfully, the passengers on that flight were under the watch of Captain Sully, a devoted pilot who'd been flying planes for over forty years. He'd wanted to fly since he was five years old.

"We're heading back to the airport," Sully told ground control.

Then he realized they couldn't make it.

"We'll head to a runway at the next airport instead," he said.

Then he realized they wouldn't make that either. The only remaining option was the Hudson River.

It was a terrifying decision to make. Only one other plane had ever landed in the river, and it had crashed, killing its pilot. No one would have blamed Sully if he'd tried to turn back to the airport, but he could see that going back just wasn't an option.

"Brace for impact," he announced over the loudspeaker.

Miraculously, Captain Sully managed to land the plane in the river. If he'd brought the plane in at an angle that was even slightly wrong, it would have broken in half, and people could have died. But everyone lived.

The crew safely managed to evacuate every passenger on board. Captain Sully was the last person off the plane.

When investigators ran a simulation of flight 1549, they found that no other pilot was capable of doing what Sully had done. But Sully's modest. He says their success was due to every member of the crew knowing their job, thinking on their feet, and working together.

Sully retired a year later. Now he spends his time giving talks throughout America about safety. He wants to make sure that, when people find themselves in emergencies, they're as prepared as they can be.

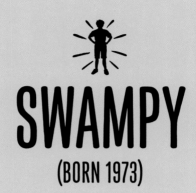

# SWAMPY
## (BORN 1973)

No one knows a lot about Daniel Hooper, better known as Swampy. All they know for sure is that he was born to a normal family, in a normal town in England, and that he cares fiercely about protecting our planet.

When the government announced their plans to build a new road through the countryside in Berkshire, people were angry. The road would mean that a lot of beautiful old oak, ash, and beech trees would be torn down.

To protest, hundreds of people, including Swampy, moved to where the new road was going to be built, and set up camps. The camps had names like Pixie Village, Heartbreak Hotel, and Rickety Bridge. The people in the camps lived together, without electricity or running water, sharing meals and foraging for food. They built houses out of wood in the trees, which they called twigloos, and wooden houses on the ground, which they called benders.

The government wasn't happy. They couldn't build their road and the delay was expensive, so they sent in people to take the protesters away.

But Swampy and his friends had another idea. They dug a maze of tunnels under the ground and hid in them. For a whole week, they lived in the tunnels until they were caught. Swampy was the last person to be found and removed.

"I feel like it's the only way to get a voice these days," he told journalists as the police led him away.

Although the protesters didn't win, they were heard. Swampy appeared on TV and radio, sharing his message of living in harmony with nature, and the government started to look at ways to avoid building new roads through ancient countryside.

# DANIEL TAMMET

## (BORN 1979)

As a baby, Daniel never stopped crying.
He would bash his head against the wall until
his mom picked him up and rocked him to sleep.
No one knew what was wrong.

Then Daniel had an epileptic fit. Everyone was terrified, because his grandfather had died of epilepsy. They thought his life was over.

Instead, it turned out that the fit had done something to Daniel's brain.

He first noticed it when his dad gave him a book about counting. Looking at the numbers, he saw more than just ones, twos, and threes. He saw images for each number. Images like crashing thunder or running water. Some numbers were lumpy, others were smooth. Some were loud and some were quiet.

As a joke, while they were playing, his brother asked him, "What's 82 x 82 x 82 x 82?"

The images twirled and spun in Daniel's head.

"45,212,176," Daniel said.

And he was right.

It didn't help Daniel to make friends in school, though. He preferred to be alone. He was diagnosed with autism and sometimes things felt overwhelming. When he needed to calm down, he would just watch the numbers go past in his head or collect ladybugs and sit between the trees.

Aside from numbers, Daniel likes languages. He can speak ten and has created his own, called Manti. He's written multiple books. And his memory isn't bad either.

"I memorized pi to 22,514 decimal places," he said, "and I am technically disabled. I just wanted to show people that disability needn't get in the way."

# TANK MAN

In the summer of 1989, thousands of students were marching through the capital of China. They were protesting against their unfair government. For years, they'd been watching the rich get richer and the poor get poorer, while those in government only looked after themselves.

As the days went on, more and more people joined the demonstrations, all meeting in a place called Tiananmen Square. Some went on hunger strike. One of China's biggest pop stars turned up to perform a concert.

The government panicked. They sent in soldiers, who shot at the protesters, killing huge numbers of them.

The next day, tanks rolled through the streets to stop anyone from protesting again.

Suddenly, the tanks came to a stop.

A man dressed in a white shirt and black trousers, clutching two shopping bags at his sides, had planted himself in front of the lead tank. When the tank tried to go around him, he stepped to the side and blocked its path again. This went on until the tank turned off its engine.

Then two men in blue appeared and led the man away.

The whole thing was captured in a photograph, and that photograph went on to become one of the most powerful symbols of resistance to injustice that we have today: one man on his own, standing up not just to a line of tanks, but to the cruel government that had put them there.

No one knows who Tank Man is or what happened to him. Some say he was arrested, some say he was killed, and some say he escaped. We may never know for sure.

# ALAN TURING

## (1912–1954)

During the Second World War, countries would speak to each other using codes to prevent their enemies from understanding their messages. The most important and difficult code was used by the Germans. It was called Enigma.

Britain desperately needed to crack it. If they could, they'd know all of their enemy's secrets, including their next moves. But it was almost impossible. There was only one person they could think of who might be able to help: Alan Turing.

Alan had loved numbers ever since he was a child. He wasn't encouraged at school, but when he got to college, Alan flourished. He was studying pure mathematics, then his unusual way of thinking led him to look for practical ways of using math. He wanted to change the way people lived in a useful manner. He published a paper that signaled the beginning of modern computers.

Once the government had brought him in, Alan helped them break the Enigma code by building a machine called the Bombe. Some people think that, by cracking the code, Alan shortened the war by four years, which would mean he saved millions of lives.

In 1952, police heard rumors that he was gay. At the time, being gay was still a crime, and he was arrested.

Alan was found guilty. Even after what he'd done for the country, he was given the choice of jail or taking drugs that would supposedly change him. He chose the drugs and they made him sick. It hurt so much that he poisoned himself and died.

But he was never forgotten. Sixty-one years later, in 2013, Alan was granted a posthumous royal pardon, and four years after that, in 2017, Turing's Law was passed, pardoning all men who had ever been convicted of anything related to being gay. His great niece, Rachel Barnes, thinks it's tremendous, but wants people to remember that Alan was a lot more than just his sexuality. He was an incredibly intelligent, devoted, and forward-thinking person who helped save the lives of countless others.

# JOHN TYNDALL

## (1820–1893)

Almost every day after school, John would walk home with his teacher, Master Conwill. They discussed geometry as they went and would stop to scratch diagrams into the dirt and snow of County Carlow, Ireland.

During his childhood in Ireland, John discovered his love of nature, and this only grew when he moved abroad to study science; he never felt more alive than when he was scaling daunting mountain slopes or trekking across freezing glaciers.

But John's adventures weren't just to explore; he was also taking notes and gathering information. John could see that everything in nature has causes and effects, and he wanted to discover what some of those causes and effects could be.

Like, what makes the sky blue?

To work it out, John created an experiment. He had a glass tube (to act as the sky), a white light shining through it (to act as the sun), and gas, which was slowly pumped into the tube (to act as the air).

John found that the gas in the tube made the light look blue. So the sky must be blue because all the tiny particles of air up there scatter the sun's light!

And not only is blue sky caused by the Tyndall effect, but the blue of someone's eyes is, too, and so is the way you can see car headlights in fog.

As successful as he became, John never forgot Ireland or his first teacher. When Master Conwill retired, John stepped in to pay him a pension so that he could live comfortably. He even went back to his old school, where he gave a gold coin to every pupil who understood a mathematical theory.

# UYAQUQ

## (CIRCA 1860–1924)

Uyaquq belonged to an Inuit people called the Yup'ik, who roamed across Alaska. They lived together in underground houses built from grass and walrus skin, wearing clothes made from animal hides and traveling with sleds pulled by dogs.

Originally, the Yup'ik had their own religion, based around spirits, monsters, half-humans, and legendary animals. Then people from Germany came, spreading the word of Jesus and the Bible.

Uyaquq converted to Christianity with his dad and rose up through the ranks to become a leader in the Alaskan Church. He spread his beliefs throughout their valley, often winning over entire villages with his charm.

One thing that amazed Uyaquq was how the English-speaking Christians could recite whole passages from the Bible using exactly the same words each time. The Yup'ik didn't have writing, so everything they knew about Christianity had been told to them and shared by talking.

After being inspired by a dream, Uyaquq decided to create his own written language.

When a German priest discovered what Uyaquq was doing, he was amazed, and he brought him to a church where he could keep working.

Uyaquq worked for five years on his language, evolving it rapidly through five stages. It became known as Yugtun, or Alaskan Yup'ik. He'd given his people their own language that they could use to share and record their own stories.

Since then, scientists have been studying Uyaquq's writing. On his own, without any help, he managed to create a whole written language from nothing, a process that had taken entire civilizations thousands of years to achieve.

# RICK VAN BEEK

Rick's daughter, Maddy, was two months old when she was diagnosed with cerebral palsy. It would mean that she couldn't control her muscles and would have trouble with learning and thinking.

Even though Maddy couldn't talk, it had always been obvious to Rick that she loved being outside. She loved the breeze and the trees and the water. It was made especially clear when a friend pulled Maddy along in a cart during a marathon. Rick could see how happy she was. He decided to make a change.

The next day, Rick quit smoking and started exercising.

When Maddy was thirteen, he completed a triathlon with her. In a triathlon, the first leg is swimming, the second is biking, and the third is running. Rick towed Maddy in a canoe for the swimming, pulled her behind him in a trailer for the biking, and

carried her in his arms for the run. Crowds were cheering for them every step of the way. As they crossed the finish line, everyone went wild.

People tell Rick he's inspiring, but he tells them it's all Maddy. She's the one who inspired him. Together, they make up Team Maddy, and they've since completed all kinds of different races, raising money for charity along the way.

How does he do it?

"She's my heart and I'm her legs," Rick says.

# LUDWIG VAN BEETHOVEN

## (1770–1827)

Neighbors said that they would often see a small boy being pushed up to a piano by his father, and that the boy would cry as he was forced to play. They said the boy was so small he had to stand on a stool to reach the keys.

The boy was beaten by his father, locked in a basement, and kept from sleeping, even when he was so tired he could barely keep his eyes open.

At school, things weren't much better. The boy had dyslexia, which meant he struggled with words. For him, music always came much more easily and, despite the harsh treatment from his father, he couldn't wait to get back and lose himself in it.

The boy got older and became a man. He wrote new music every day, hardly lifting his hands off the piano. Even as an adult, though, he was so shy it hurt, and that shyness kept him from ever getting married or having children.

One day, the man discovered that he was going deaf. It threw him into a deep, dark sadness. How would he compose music if he couldn't hear? And what would he do if he couldn't compose music?

Amazingly, even when he lost his hearing completely, the man carried on writing music. In fact, he composed some of his most beautiful music without being able to hear at all.

The boy that cried on to the piano, and the man that he became, was named Ludwig van Beethoven, and he's considered by many people to be the greatest composer who ever lived.

# VINCENT VAN GOGH

## (1853–1890)

Growing up, Vincent didn't have any confidence and he had no idea what he wanted to be. He tried being a preacher, working in a bookstore, and traveling as a salesman, but none of them worked out.

Then Vincent decided he would become a painter.

He went to Paris and met the famous artists of the time: Gauguin and Monet. He tried to copy their styles, but couldn't, so he invented his own way of painting instead.

At the time, Vincent was struggling with his feelings. He couldn't sleep. He barely ate. Often, he got confused and upset by the world around him. One night, he chased his friend with a razor and ended up cutting his own ear off instead. Worried, his brother sent him to a hospital to try and get better.

Vincent painted the sadness and madness that he felt inside him and the beauty and inspiration that he found around him. He painted the golden sunflowers and the swirling night sky. He painted himself, cold and confused.

His paintings were dramatic, beautiful, and emotional. They were also a completely unique and new way of painting, discovered by him looking inside himself instead of at others.

While he was alive, Vincent only ever sold one painting, and not for a lot of money. Now he's considered one of the best and most original painters who ever lived. Today, buying one of his paintings would cost you as much as buying an entire island.

# NICK VUJICIC

## (BORN 1982)

Nick likes skydiving, soccer, and swimming. He paints. He writes books. He was even featured on the cover of *Surfer* magazine after he became the first person in history to do 360-degree spins on his board.

Nick was also born with no arms and no legs.

Doctors were shocked when his mother gave birth to him; they hadn't been prepared for Nick's condition and couldn't understand what had caused it.

Growing up, Nick was unhappy. He felt alone and angry. It didn't seem fair that he'd been given a different body than everyone else and he was worried that he'd never be able to live the way he wanted to. He wondered what the point of everything was. He wondered what he was supposed to do with his life.

Then, one day, Nick read an article about a disabled man who had inspired thousands of people through his speeches about overcoming adversity. He decided he wanted to try it, too. For his first talk, he spoke to a hall of three hundred fourteen-year-old students. He was so nervous, he was shaking. But after a few minutes, most of the students were in tears. One girl raised her hand.

"I'm so sorry to interrupt," she said, "but could I come and hug you?"

As they hugged, she whispered in his ear that no one had ever told her she was beautiful the way she was, which is what Nick had said to all the children in the room.

From then on, Nick knew what he wanted to do. He has traveled across forty-four countries, giving over three thousand talks. Everywhere he goes, he inspires and moves people. He lets them know that they are all loved and beautiful, even when they feel like they're not.

"It's a lie to think you're not good enough," he says. "It's a lie to think you're not worth anything."

# TAIKA WAITITI

## (BORN 1975)

Taika always loved comic books and superheroes,
but he never saw people like himself in them.

His father is Maori, which is the name given to the first people who lived on the islands of New Zealand. The Maori people have their own rich culture, language, and beliefs. They practice arts like carving, dancing, singing, and facial tattooing, and believe that we are all descended from two original gods, the Sky Father and the Earth Mother.

Despite their culture and history, Taika always felt like they were never properly represented in films and TV. Whenever Maori characters appeared, they had to be tough guys or warriors, they were never funny, and they never felt real.

"We never embraced the buffoons in our culture," Taika said. "Maori nerds or Maori dorks."

So that's what he set out to do.

Taika wrote and directed a film about a young Maori boy who adores Michael Jackson, misses his dad, and spends a lot of time talking to his pet goat. Then he directed another film, *Hunt for the Wilderpeople*, about a Maori boy who loves hip-hop and ends up running from the police, in the forest, with a grumpy old man.

Both films were hilarious and heartbreaking, and they caught the attention of people all over the world. Because of them, Taika was asked to direct a big Hollywood superhero movie titled *Thor*, about the god of thunder and his quest to stop the destruction of civilization. Taika has shown the world another side to Maori people and he's been able to create his own comic-book universe, too.

# AI WEIWEI

## (BORN 1957)

Imagine yourself in a blank, gray room as big as a cathedral. And imagine that the room contains one hundred million sunflower seeds. Now imagine that, instead of sprouting from sunflowers, each of those seeds had to be handmade and painted by an actual person.

What you've just pictured in your mind is one of Ai Weiwei's most famous pieces of art. To him, it's one piece of art made of millions of pieces of art, the same way China is one country made of 1.3 billion citizens, and we're one species of 7 billion people.

Ai says that the purpose of art is to fight for freedom. In China, where he's from, people often aren't granted the freedoms people in other countries are used to. For example, when Ai started criticizing the government on his blog, it was shut down, and they started spying on him by listening in to his phone calls and following him through the streets.

Ai spoke out through art when an earthquake killed thousands of children in China. To save money, the government had built the schools so badly that they came crashing down as the ground shook, trapping the children inside.

Then, when police beat him up for letting everyone know, he made art from the scans the hospital took of his brain.

Ai wasn't allowed to leave his house, his art studio was burned down, and he was even imprisoned for eighty-one days. To show how furious he was at the government, he filmed himself smashing an eight-hundred-year-old Chinese pot worth one million dollars!

"I speak out for people around me who are afraid," said Ai.

Why?

Because we're all tiny sunflower seeds, but we're all part of something bigger, too.

# OSCAR WILDE

## (1854–1900)

Isola Wilde died unexpectedly a few days before her tenth birthday. Her brother, Oscar, was devastated. Not knowing what else to do, he spent long periods of time sitting by her grave and telling her stories.

As he grew older, Oscar became a famous poet and playwright and was often seen wandering around dressed in strange clothes and wearing huge flowers. He was known everywhere for being hilarious, confident, and loud, but people said that if he ever started talking about his sister, which he often did, he'd get quieter and softer.

One of his most famous poems was written for her; the first lines are:

*Tread lightly, she is near*

*Under the snow,*

*Speak gently, she can hear*

*The daisies grow.*

Oscar was gay, and he fell in love with a young lord whose father was cruel and intolerant. Because of him, Oscar was brought to trial, found guilty, and sentenced to two years of hard labor in prison. When he got out, Oscar moved straight to France. He was sick and poor, and he died a few years later. It wasn't until after his death that his writing was really noticed. Since then, his plays and poems have been performed, studied, and filmed all over the world.

Visitors to his tomb used to cover their mouths in lipstick and leave bright kisses all over it until a glass case was put up. They would sit and speak to Oscar the way he used to sit and speak to his little sister.

"We are all in the gutter," he once said, "but some of us are looking at the stars."

# NICHOLAS WINTON

## (1909–2015)

### In December 1938, Nicholas's friend called to cancel their ski trip.

"We should go to Prague instead," his friend said. "There's something you have to see."

What Nicholas saw when he got there were hundreds of thousands of refugees who'd escaped from Germany. Most of them were Jewish. They were fleeing because the Nazis who controlled Germany had been hunting them down, taking them to camps, and killing them, just because of their religion. In Prague, they had no money, no food, nowhere to live, and nowhere to go.

Nicholas knew he had to at least try to do something.

From a hotel room, he started taking names, photos, and details of children so that he could help get them into England. Once he got back to London, he worked at fundraising for the children and searching for families who could take them in.

By August 1939, Nicholas had managed to get 669 children into Britain. A month later, all German borders closed, and most of the families the children had left behind were killed by the Nazis.

Nobody really knew what Nicholas had done until fifty years later. His wife found a book in the attic with all the names of the children in it, and she asked a TV show for help tracking them down. Nicholas was invited on the TV show. He didn't know why he was there—his wife and the TV people hadn't told him—and he didn't know what to expect.

While he was sitting in the audience, the presenter said, "Stand up if you owe your life to Nicholas Winton!"

All of the people sitting around Nicholas stood up.

They were adults now and they had him to thank for that.

# KEN YEANG

## (BORN 1948)

Ken was four when his father took him to see the house he was building for their family. He would never forget it.

When it came time to choose a college major, Ken's father pushed him to study medicine and become a doctor. But he had never lost his fascination with buildings, and he persuaded his father to let him study architecture instead.

It was the 1970s. Ken became one of the first people to focus on ecological design, which means architecture that works with the nature. His idea was to create buildings that merged and worked with the natural world instead of demolishing and replacing it.

His buildings harness the wind for ventilation, use the sun for heat and light, catch rain for cooling, and are filled to the brim with lush gardens and overflowing terraces of native plants. By adding these gardens, Ken tries to keep the buildings from looking like random lumps of metal and glass dropped on to the surface

of the planet. He wants them to be tied to nature. He wants the buildings to be alive.

Ken's own house is called the Roof-Roof House, and it incorporates all of these elements. When he first built it, other architects made fun of him.

"Don't hire Ken," they'd tell people, pointing at the Roof-Roof House. "He'll build you something weird, like that."

These days, people think of the house as being ahead of its time, and they look to it as an example of what to work toward.

A newspaper recently named Ken as one of the fifty people who could save our planet. He still thinks that the most important thing about any new building is that it makes people happy.

Funky Chicken
I De Rap Guy
U.N. (United Neighbours)
All You Sea
I Luv Me Mudder
Thought For Monday
Voices For Choice
De Magic Poem
The Vegans
Play Daze
Before All These Cities
Serious Luv
Fearless Bushmen
Him In The Himalayas

# BENJAMIN ZEPHANIAH

## (BORN 1958)

Benjamin could barely read or write when he was kicked out of school. He was only thirteen. Things had been so hard at home that he found it difficult to care about studying and always ended up in trouble.

What he really cared about was poetry. Not old poems by dead poets, but the living poems and stories that his mother told him about life in Jamaica. Ones like the tales of Anansi, a tricky spider who could disguise himself as a man, who made a deal with the sky-God to own all of the stories in the world.

Benjamin knew what he wanted to do, so he started doing it.

He wrote his own poems and performed them wherever he could: in churches, community centers, and on the street.

Soon, people started listening.

His poetry was for real people and it was about real things, like the pain of racism, the joy of dancing, and whether it's okay to eat animals. In no time, you could hear it everywhere: dance floors, protests, concerts, and on the TV. His mission was to bring poetry back to life, to remind people of the power it still has. Benjamin traveled the world, reciting his verses over music that was a mixture of everything from hip-hop to rock.

As he went, he inspired young people not just to write, but to rap, to perform, and to speak up for what they believed in.

Benjamin has helped prime ministers, been on worldwide tours, written bestselling books, and can hardly walk down the street in London without people calling out to him.

"Thanks!" they shout.

He waves back.

And it's all down to poetry.

**BEN BROOKS**

was born in 1992 and lives in Berlin. He is the author of several books, including *Grow Up* and *Lolito*, which won the Somerset Maugham Award in 2015.

**QUINTON WINTER**

is a British illustrator, artist, and colorist. He has worked for many clients including the *Guardian* newspaper, Walker Books, "Gogglebox," *2000AD*, Vertigo Comics, *Mojo*, and the BBC.

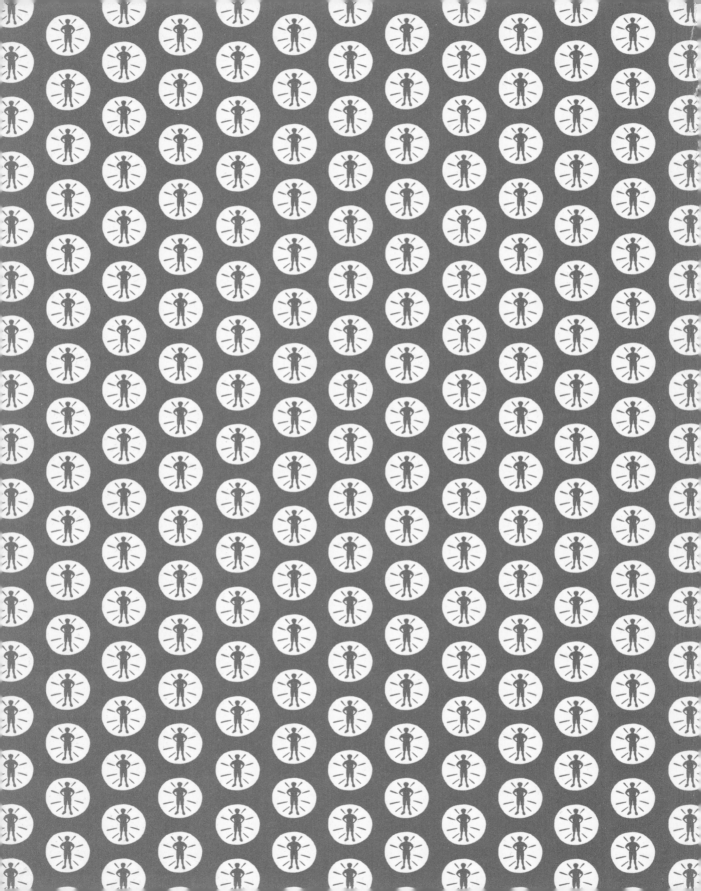